THE ROLE OF MEDIATION IN RESOLVING INDIA–PAKISTAN CONFLICT: PARAMETERS AND POSSIBILITIES

The Regional Centre for Strategic Studies (RCSS) is an independent, non-profit and non-governmental organization for collaborative research, networking and interaction on strategic and international issues pertaining to South Asia. Set up in 1992, the RCSS is based in Colombo, Sri Lanka.

The RCSS is a South Asian forum for studies, training and multi-track dialogue and deliberation on issues of regional interest. All activities of RCSS are designed with a South Asia focus and are usually participated by experts from all South Asian countries. The Centre is envisaged as a forum for advancing the cause of cooperation, security, conflict resolution, confidence building, peace and development in the countries of the South Asian region.

The RCSS serves its South Asian and international constituency by: (a) networking programmes that promote interaction, communication and exchange between institutions and individuals within and outside the region engaged in South Asian strategic studies; (b) organizing regional workshops and seminars and sponsoring and coordinating collaborative research; and (c) disseminating output of the research through publications which include books, monographs and a quarterly newsletter. The RCSS facilitates scholars and other professionals of South Asia to address, mutually and collectively, problems and issues of topical interest for all countries of the region.

Queries may be addressed to:

Regional Centre for Strategic Studies
2 Elibank Road
Colombo 5
SRI LANKA
Tel: (94-11) 2599734, 2599735
Fax: 2599993; e-mail: rcss@sri.lanka.net
RCSS website: http://www.rcss.org

RCSS Policy Studies 29

The Role of Mediation in Resolving India-Pakistan Conflict: Parameters and Possibilities

AMIT DHOLAKIA

REGIONAL CENTRE FOR STRATEGIC STUDIES
COLOMBO

MANOHAR
2005

Published by
Ajay Kumar Jain for
Manohar Publishers & Distributors
4753/23 Ansari Road, Daryaganj
New Delhi 110 002
and
Regional Centre for Strategic Studies
2 Elibank Road
Colombo 5
SRI LANKA
Tel: (94-11) 2599734-5; Fax: 2599993;
e-mail: rcss@sri.lanka.net
Website: http://www.rcss.org

First published 2005

Views expressed in materials published in *RCSS Policy Studies* are those of the contributors, and not necessarily of the Regional Centre for Strategic Studies.

ISBN 81-7304-629-8

Typeset by
Kohli Print
Delhi 110 051

Printed at
Lordson Publishers Pvt. Ltd.
Delhi 110 007

Distributed in South Asia by
FOUNDATION BOOKS
4381/4, Ansari Rorad
Daryaganj, New Delhi 110 002
and its branches at Mumbai, Hyderabad,
Bangalore, Chennai, Kolkata

Contents

RCSS is grateful to the
Ford Foundation for its generous
support for the Kodikara Award
on which this report is based.

Acknowledgements

I feel privileged to put on record the contributions of several persons to the successful completion of this study. I am particularly grateful to Prof. Dilip H. Mohite, Research Supervisor, for his scholarly guidance and encouragement in my endeavours. The Regional Centre for Strategic Studies, Colombo, especially former Executive Director Maj. Gen. Dipankar Banerji (retd.), present Executive Director, Prof. Sridhar K. Khatri, and former Programme Officer Ms. Minna Thaheer deserve very special and sincere thanks for their valuable institutional support and forbearance during the course of this study.

AMIT DHOLAKIA

CHAPTER 1

Introduction
Objectives and Scope of the Study

THE POST-COLD WAR SECURITY ENVIRONMENT

The international system experienced a qualitative transformation following the series of processes sweeping across the world after the disintegration of the Soviet Union and the communist bloc towards the end of the 1980s. The policy makers, scholars and students of international politics have been compelled to recast their habitual modes of thinking to make sense out of the turbulence and promise of the emerging world order. A unipolar world order dominated by the United States-led alliance of some Western capitalist states has replaced the bipolarity of the Cold War era. Commanding forces of globalization, erosion of state sovereignty, extensive economic interdependence, uniform trade and tariff policies enforced by the transnational institutions, technological linkages among states, increased flow of information across geographical boundaries, international social networking through means of advanced communication and information technologies, raise mind-boggling possibilities about the future of mankind.

The security environment of this emerging world order is characterized by paradoxes. Due to the altered perceptions and issues that caused conflicts during the Cold War era, the risk of a worldwide military clash has reduced. This has impelled the US and Russia to agree to slash their nuclear and conventional weapons' arsenals in a phased manner. However, such arms reductions have not contributed to an increased sense of security as the transnational challenges of terrorism, proliferation of weapons of mass destruction, violent ethnic conflicts and environmental crises pose threats as serious as those posed by militaries and weapons. Research on new laser weapons and space-based missile shields continue to enjoy high priority in America's defence planning. The arms industries and military exports of the weapons-producing states have also largely remained unaffected by the end of the Cold War.

The contemporary regional security environment also exhibits apparent contradictions. Cold War compulsions exacerbated regional conflicts and restricted the ability of international organizations to resolve them. The end of the Cold War was, therefore, seen by many as increasing the ability of the international community to resolve conflicts.[1] The advantages of reduced international tension have also reached different regions that were caught in deadly conflicts during the Cold War era. Serious attempts to mend fences between adversarial states in Latin America, the Middle East and the Far East have been undertaken, albeit with varying degrees of success. The US brokered a peace agreement after decades of violent conflict in Northern Ireland. Vietnam disengaged from Cambodia and launched initiatives for normalization of relations with China. Vietnam, which had remained isolated from its neighbourhood of South-East Asia, has joined the ASEAN. South America's traditional rivals, Argentina and Brazil, agreed to freeze their nuclear programmes and open their nuclear facilities to inspection by the International Atomic Energy Agency. The Cuban withdrawal from Angola and the thawing of the long-deadlocked relationship between the two Koreas are some other indicators of the propitious effects of the post-Cold War strategic transformation on the regional and subregional security orders.

However, it can also be argued forcefully that in the new world order, the international community will be less capable of resolving inter-state conflicts in different regions than it was in earlier

[1] Andrew Bennett and Joseph Lepgold, 'Reinventing Collective Security after the Cold War and Gulf Conflict', *Political Science Quarterly*, vol. 108, no. 2, 1993, pp. 213–37; Edward A. Kolodziej and Roger E. Kanet (eds.), *Coping with Conflict after the Cold War*, Baltimore: Johns Hopkins University Press, 1996.

times.[2] Unaffected by the global shift, several areas are in the grip of ethnic insurgencies, intra-state clashes, militarization, arms races, xenophobia, terrorism and religious fundamentalism today. The persisting preoccupation of parts of Asia and Africa with their old enmities is a cause of concern and seems in-congruous with the orientation of the rest of the world engaged in a race for economic growth. Regional arms control, conflict resolution or confidence-building endeavours have eluded several inter-state conflicts. The fierce conflicts in the Balkans, civil wars in Somalia, Sudan, Sri Lanka, Chechnya, and the escalation of the India-Pakistan conflict are some illustrations of the destabilizing conditions of the current age. America's wars against Afghanistan and Iraq and the forced regime change brought about in these two states in 2001 and 2003, respectively signify the direction and quality of the international order in the coming years.

THE PERSISTING INDIA-PAKISTAN CONFLICT

Few would deny that the intractable conflict between India and Pakistan is one of the most dangerous conflicts in the world today. The two states have been involved in a relationship of unrelenting hostility ever since their independence from British rule, fighting three full-scale wars in 1947–8, 1965 and 1971, a semi-war in 1999, and coming very close to war in 1955, 1987, 1990, 2001 and 2002. The roller-coaster ride of their relationship—short-lived ups but prolonged downs—defies all attempts at conflict management and resolution. The Cold War mindset, as reflected in zero-sum game scenarios, conception of conflict as one of the fundamental values, and a nuclear arms race still seems to hold sway over the majority of the people, decision makers and commentators in the Indian subcontinent.

[2] Andrew Hurrell, 'Collective Security and International Order Revisited', *International Relations*, vol. 11, no. 1, April 1992, pp. 37–56; John L. Gaddis, 'Threat Illusions, the Long Peace, and the Future of the International System', in Charles W. Kegley Jr. (ed.), *The Long Postwar Peace*, New York: HarperCollins, 1991, pp. 25–55; Richard K. Betts, 'The Delusion of Impartial Intervention', *Foreign Affairs*, vol. 73, November/December 1994, pp. 20–33.

There have been many disputes between India and Pakistan since their independence, such as over the division of assets, left-over property of evacuees, accession of princely states, distribution of river water resources, and so on. Some of these issues have also been settled amicably through negotiations. However, Jammu & Kashmir has remained the basic issue of India–Pakistan conflict. This conflict is not merely a state-level conflict: it goes beyond the apparent issues of politics, territory, strategy or diplomacy. It is so deep-seated in the social psychology of the two states that their societies also actively participate in the episodes and processes of conflicts. The fact that the two countries have maintained diplomatic contacts at different levels and even cooperated in several areas has not succeeded in dispelling the overpowering sense of insecurity and fear in the subcontinent. No wonder, the mood today is quite sullen about the prospects of peace in South Asia.

India's and Pakistan's obsession with the pursuit of their conflict defies logic. Both countries are placed among some of the least developed states of the world. Their scarce resources, which ought to have been used for providing basic amenities to the people, are wantonly diverted towards defence-related expenditure. South Asia, which contains more than one and a half billion people (about one-fourth of humanity) and is home to some great civilizations of the world, stands out for its pathetic human development indicators. Illiteracy, poverty, unemployment, inadequate health-care facilities, malnourishment, infant mortality, and atrocities against women are endemic to India and Pakistan. Uneven development, ecological deterioration, political instability, deficiencies in democratic structures and ethnic sub-nationalisms further complicate the conflict between these two states.

With a population of about 144 million, Pakistan has a high infant mortality rate of 76 per 1,000 live births, a literacy rate of 41 per cent, per capita national income of $420, and external debt of $26.5 billion. Its average annual GDP growth rate has hovered between 2.5 and 4 per cent during the last decade.[3] With more

[3] World Development Indicators, World Bank Database, April 2002.

than one billion people, India also has a high infant mortality rate of 65 per 1,000 live births, a literacy rate of 61 per cent, external debt of $83 billion, and per capita national income of $470.[4] It has grown at an average rate of about 6 per cent in recent years.

Advances in military technology and increase in the intensity of warfare today have raised the costs of fighting a war manifold. While the three-month war with Pakistan in 1947–8 cost India only Rs. 2 crore [1 crore equals 10 million], even a short-lived war today will prove economically ruinous for both countries. According to one estimate, a 1,000-hour war (or a 41.6-day war, to be precise) will cost India approximately Rs. 27,000 crore. The cost of military operations in the highly localized Kargil conflict between India and Pakistan in 1999 was estimated at more than Rs. 5,000 crore by a commentator.[5] Even the human costs of any future India–Pakistan war could be severe, even unthinkable, considering the advanced weaponry in the possession of the two states and the risk of use of nuclear capability. According to a study by the Indian think tank Strategic Foresight Group of the International Center for Peace Initiatives, if terrorism in Kashmir is not contained, the state will see the death of 6,000 civilians, 10,000 terrorists and 2,500 security personnel between 2004 and 2008. The Siachen glacier conflict alone would cost (in Indian rupees) Rs. 72 billion for India and Rs. 18 billion for Pakistan, and cause the death of about 1,500 soldiers by 2009. If the troops are mobilized again on the pattern of 2002 for a year, it will cost India 0.46 per cent of GDP and Pakistan 2.25 per cent of GDP.[6]

It is uncertain if improved development and diversion of resources for the welfare sector from the defence outlay would make the India–Pakistan conflict more moderate. But a more educated, satisfied and healthy citizenry certainly makes for a society capable of understanding conflicts, and organizing conflict resolution and peace. In view of the human, economic and social costs of India–Pakistan conflict and the associated nuclear risks, it is in

[4] Ibid.

[5] Shrikant Rao, 'The Price of War', *Sunday Mid-day* (Mumbai), 4 July 1999.

[6] Ilmas Fatehuli and Semu Bhatt, *The Cost of Conflict between India and Pakistan*, Mumbai: International Center for Peace Initiatives/Strategic Foresight Group, 2004.

the vital interest not merely of the people of the two states, but also of the entire world to work towards conflict prevention, peace and stability in South Asia. Among the several approaches to conflict resolution, mediation has also been proposed and applied as a method of peace building between India and Pakistan in the tumultous history of their relationship.

FRAMEWORK OF INTERNATIONAL MEDIATION

Theories of conflict resolution do not look upon conflict as a negative and insoluble phenomenon. They redefine it as a problem to be settled by following a broad range of strategies and techniques that do not involve force or violence: mediation, negotiation, arbitration, conciliation, confidence building, referendum, informal consensus, cooperative living experience, interfaith movement, limited disarmament, etc. Conflict resolution cannot be brought about by a single approach but by several processes operating simultaneously, sometimes parallel to, or sometimes in conjunction with each other.

Third-party intervention is a common response to any human conflict. In the range of methods of third-party intervention, international mediation is considered important for prevention, management, and resolution of international conflicts. International mediation has been applied in several conflicts in the post-World War II period. It has been used extensively to manage conflicts in the Balkans, the Middle East and Africa in recent times. Mediation has also been applied between India and Pakistan to help the two states resolve their disputes.

Though international mediation has been practised for long, organized and rigorous research on this form of dispute resolution began only after World War II. Nevertheless, a substantial corpus of conceptual and empirical knowledge on the process, components and effectiveness of international mediation now exists due to the pioneering works of scholars like John W. Burton, William I. Zartman, Jacob Bercovitch, Jeffrey Rubin, Saadia Touval, Ronald Fisher, D. Frei, and O.R. Young.

OBJECTIVES OF THE STUDY

Systematic analysis of international mediation as an approach to conflict management and resolution between India and Pakistan is conspicuous by its near-absence from the academic discourse in South Asia. The debate on the role of mediation in India–Pakistan relations has rarely been well-informed or well-argued. Hence, the relevance and applicability of a third-party role needs to be researched and understood in a disciplined and analytical fashion. The few writings that exist on the history of mediation between India and Pakistan are mostly narratives of the mediation episodes, and not explicitly carried out with an analytical orientation. Interestingly, a good number of these contributions have been in the form of articles in popular magazines and newspapers; only a few are of academic nature. A theoretically cogent, comprehensive and single-author study on the applicability of mediation between India and Pakistan is still awaited.

The present exploratory enquiry attempts to make a contribution to the understanding of the India–Pakistan conflict by cataloguing the involvement of third parties in it and analysing the potential of and constraints on such involvement in future. In the light of the distinctive nature and conditions of the India–Pakistan conflict, the present study interrogates how far, in what form, and to what effect this conflict has lent itself to a third-party role in the past, and what essential preconditions and contextual factors impeded or assisted such a role.

Peace in South Asia cannot be interpreted as a static condition, but as a process of continuous and constructive management of differences between states. Though conflict avoidance is the primary challenge to India–Pakistan relations, this study cannot remain restricted to the problem of conflict avoidance only. Indeed, crisis prevention, conflict avoidance, conflict management, and conflict resolution are ascending and successive steps of a larger process of peacemaking between two adversaries. Mapping the domain of international mediation as a contested concept, this study will examine the link between mediation and conflict resolution and indicate the preferable direction of an international role in the India–Pakistan conflict. The present enquiry is conceptually embedded in the accumulated knowledge relating to international conflict resolution. Though fully alert to the theorizing concerning conflict resolution and mediation, this research is not primarily theoretical in substance, i.e. it is not theory-verifying or theory-generating research. Being an evaluative and qualitative enquiry, it might add, in a tangential way, to the theoretical understanding of the India–Pakistan conflict.

KEY RESEARCH QUESTIONS

The following are the key research questions raised and investigated in this study:

1. What is the history of third-party involvement in the India–Pakistan conflict? Who has carried out these initiatives and with what effect?
2. What is the function of international mediation in the management and resolution of the conflict between India and Pakistan? To what extent, and in what manner, has mediation influenced the security environment in South Asia?
3. What kind of costs and benefits do India and Pakistan see in mediation? What are the arguments for and against international mediation in the India–Pakistan conflict?
4. Under what conditions can mediation be applied gainfully in the India–Pakistan conflict? What are the constraints on its application?
5. What changes are required in the application of third-party involvement in the India–Pakistan conflict?

CHAPTER 2

Conceptual Foundations and Background of Mediation in International Conflicts

THE IMPERATIVE OF CONFLICT MANAGEMENT AND RESOLUTION

Conflicts are an inevitable and unavoidable part of life. We have been experiencing varied forms of conflict from the beginning of mankind. Conflicts occur whenever two parties are unable to achieve commonly desired goals at the same time. They can occur at several levels: inter-personal, inter-group, inter-societal, and international. The number of conflicts in the world have been increasing and becoming more violent, complicated, sophisticated and widespread with passage of time. Hence, total elimination of conflicts is impossible to achieve. No institution or effort can eradicate the natural instincts of selfishness, violence, envy, acquisitiveness and competition that lie at the root of all conflicts.

However, social and political history tells us that even as human conflicts cannot be eradicated, they can be managed, settled, resolved or transformed through appropriate actions and arrangements. One can strive to mitigate the underlying causes that create conflicts and motivate human beings and their associations not to use violence for obtaining their goals. The institution of the State also evolved from the urge to apply some form of conflict settlement and resolution mechanism in an anarchical situation. The progress of civilizations and societies is basically a process of establishing and legitimizing conflict resolving mechanisms.

Conflicts are not static but dynamic; they have a life-cycle. Each conflict moves through stages of this cycle. Conflict prevention, conflict management and conflict resolution are interrelated steps in a larger peace process between two adversaries. In this cyclical concept of conflict, *conflict management* means eliminating the violent or violence-ridden means of pursuing the conflict, while *conflict resolution* means mitigating the causes of a conflict between parties and eliminating the sources of incompatibility in their positions. A conflict can be resolved only when a mutually consistent set of actions is worked out, and when all the involved parties accept the solution as fair.[1] Conflict resolution, thus, explicitly focuses on the underlying sources of a conflict, as well as on the terms of settlement.

International conflicts can be of several types: strategic, territorial, trade, ideological, power, resource conflicts. There have been the most violent and obdurate conflicts in recent times. The wars of the twentieth century (World War I, World War II, the Korean war, the Arab-Israeli conflicts, the India–Pakistan conflict, the Vietnam war, the Yugoslavia–NATO war, etc.) resulted in the death of 30 million persons.[2] The unprecedented destruction of life and property wrought by World War II raised political and moral questions about the nature of the international system and its propensity to promote war. The invention of nuclear weapons and their use in Hiroshima and Nagasaki by the United States alerted thinking people about the potential for annihilation through nuclear weapons. In modern wars, the victors and the vanquished suffer equally. The possibility of nuclear annihilation as a consequence of the doctrine of Mutually Assured Destruction makes war between the great powers an act of collective suicide. While nuclear warheads represent the ultimate in human violence, the killing power of conventional, chemical, and biological weapons also has the potential for producing unmitigated human suffering.

Although informal attempts to control and resolve international conflicts date back to the origin of the sovereign State system, the international community has been seriously engaged in thinking

[1] Michael Nicholson, *Conflict Analysis*, London: English Universities Press, 1971.
[2] *Economist*, 9 November 1999.

about efforts at controlling wars and conflicts since the end of World War I. Diverse experiments and methods to reduce the probability of violence among states have been tried. The League of Nations, the UN, the International Court of Justice (ICJ), and international law and covenants, are some of the institutional and legal mechanisms for control of conflicts. Such institutional and legal mechanisms did not meet with universal approval initially, as they were set up by the victorious dominant powers and structured in accordance with their priorities and interests. Nevertheless, they provided the welcome first steps in an anarchical world where arrangements for global governance and conflict resolution were weak. Horrified by the unprecedented destruction wrought by World War II, the prospects of accelerated superpower rivalry and proliferation of nuclear weapons, the discipline of international relations also began focusing on international conflicts and ways of resolving them. Governments also took the lead in some cases in instituting conflict resolution centres and sponsoring conflict-research at academic institutions.

THIRD-PARTY METHODS OF CONFLICT MANAGEMENT AND RESOLUTION

It would be ideal if the conflicting parties were able to negotiate a settlement through their own efforts. However, this does not happen in all conflicts due to a variety of reasons. Hence, third-party methods of conflict management and resolution are used where parties' own initiatives for settlement have failed and the conflict has lingered on for a long period of time. Mediation has been the most established and accepted form of third-party intervention in international conflicts. Settlement of many major conflicts in the post-World War II period was an outcome of mediation by third parties. The end of the war between Iran and Iraq (1988) and between Morocco and Western Sahara (1997) was brought about through UN mediation. The UN also mediated the Geneva Accord in 1989 between the US and the USSR which terminated the Afghanistan conflict resulting from the Soviet invasion of that country. The Camp David Accord between Egypt and Israel (1978), as well as the Israel–PLO Accords (1993 and 1995) became possible due to third-party mediation.

Forms of Third-Party Involvement

The method of intervention chosen by a third party can take several forms depending upon the character of the conflict, the motives of the intervening party, and the interests of the disputants. Third-party intervention, therefore, covers a wide spectrum ranging from facilitation and consultation to binding arbitration. The following major techniques of third-party intervention have been tried in interstate disputes.

Adjudication

Adjudication is a judicial procedure of settling disputes between states. The International Court of Justice (ICJ) at The Hague, established in 1945 by Chapter XIV of the UN Charter, is the foremost adjudicating institution at the international level. The ICJ was an improved version of the Permanent Court of International Justice established by the League of Nations in 1921. The court rules on the basis of the provisions of international law, relevant treaties, international agreements, customary international law, and accepted legal principles. The verdict of the international court is non-binding on the parties, which retain their sovereign right to reject it. Adjudication is an attempt to enforce a system of legal accountability to deter states from treating their international contractual obligations lightly, and provide reparations in case of violations. It can be advantageous inasmuch as it provides impartial, impersonal, principled, orderly and depoliticized procedures of conflict resolution. Adjudication also reinforces the idea of the rule of law at the international level.

Some of the examples of successful cases of conflict resolution through the ICJ are: the US–Norway case over territorial waters and fishing rights involving British fishing vessels operating in the waters claimed by Norway (1951), the North Sea Continental Shelf cases (1969) involving Denmark, the Netherlands, and West Germany over the drilling of oil and gas in the North Sea. More recently, the ICJ settled the dispute between Burkina Faso and Mali in the Frontier Dispute case of 1986.

Arbitration

Arbitration is a formal and quasi-judicial process. It is a 'procedure whereby a third party holds a hearing, at which time the disputants state their positions on the issues, call witnesses and offer supportive evidence for their respective positions. After evaluating the evidence and considering other relevant factors (e.g. legal constraints and economic conditions), the third party issues a binding settlement.'[3]

Arbitration involves 'a legitimate and authoritative third party who renders a binding judgement to the parties that is arrived at by considering the merits of the opposing positions and imposing a settlement deemed to be fair'.[4]

Arbitration has been used for settling international as well as internal conflicts for long. The ancient Greek city states had institutionalized the procedure of arbitration. The Pope also acted as an arbitrator between European states during medieval times.[5] The Hague Convention for the Pacific Settlement of International Disputes (1899) gave formal recognition to arbitration for settlement of disputes. Arbitration can be relevant if the dispute concerns the interpretation of the provisions of treaties, or minor claims on territory and distribution of natural resources. It is widely used in commercial conflicts at both domestic and international levels. Arbitration is unsuitable for protracted and

[3] F. Elkouri and E. Elkouri, *How Arbitration Works*, Washington: BNA Books, 1997, cited by William H. Ross, 'Hybrid Forms of Third-Party Dispute Resolution: Theoretical Implications of Combining Mediation', *Academy of Management Review*, vol. 25, no. 2, April 2000, p. 417.

[4] Ronald J. Fisher, 'Pacific, Impartial, Third-Party Intervention in International Conflict: A Review and an Analysis', in John A. Vasquez, Stanford Jaffe, James Turner Johnson and Linda Stamato (eds.), *Beyond Confrontation: Learning Conflict Resolution in the Post-Cold War Era*, Ann Arbor: University of Michigan Press, 1995, p. 41.

[5] John Burton and Frank Dukes, *Conflict: Practices in Management, Settlement and Resolution*, Houndmills and London: Macmillan, 1990, p. 102.

deep-rooted international conflicts where issues of identity or survival prevent bargaining, barter or a give-and-take approach.

In the case of arbitration between states, or between states and individuals, the Permanent Court of Arbitration and the International Center for the Settlement of Investment Disputes (ICSID) are the predominant organizations. Arbitration is also used as part of the dispute settlement process under the WTO Dispute Settlement Understanding.

Conciliation

The word *conciliation* is derived from the Latin word *conciliare* which means 'to give, to call together, to overcome something together'. Conciliation:

> involves a trusted intermediary who provides an informal communication link between or among the antagonists with the purpose of identifying major issues, lowering tensions, and encouraging movement to direct interaction, most often negotiation. Related forms of intervention... are good offices, wherein the intermediary acts as an unofficial go-between and fact-finding, wherein the third party assesses the conflict and provides a statement or report back to the parties.[6]

Unlike *mediation*, which offers active assistance in resolving a conflict, *conciliation* indicates only a preliminary involvement of an outside party with agenda setting, record keeping, and communication. Conciliation is essentially a psychological process involving third-party efforts to improve the relationship between disputants; correct misunderstandings; promote empathy for each other's attitudes, emotions and needs; and reduce fear and distrust. The Neemrana dialogue process between the Indian and Pakistani delegates under the auspices of the United States Information Service in the early 1990s was an example of conciliation.

Consultation

Consultation means facilitative analysis by a knowledgeable and trusted third party who evaluates the conflict situation and helps

[6] Fisher, 'Pacific, Impartial, Third Party Intervention', p. 40.

develop creative alternatives and solutions.[7] This form of dispute settlement is applicable more in domestic and organizational settings rather than in international relations. Occasionally, consultation has been practised in the Commonwealth of Nations, where exploratory and problem solving discussions serve the function of preparing adversaries for negotiations.[8]

Facilitation

The word *facilitation* has originated from the Latin word *facilitare* which means 'to ease'. The role of a facilitator, therefore, is to provide such support to the parties in conflict that will ease their communications, negotiations, and search for an agreement. Facilitation is the least invasive form of mediation, and is generally not resisted by disputants. Eschewing orientation towards power politics, facilitation operates in a cooperative setting and promotes integrative outcomes. Facilitation has as:

> its goal the improvement of the conflicting parties' own capabilities and resources to achieve a more creative decision-making process and resolution of the conflict.... The aim is to transform the situation from a conflict which divides the parties into a problem that they share and over which they need to cooperate if it is to be resolved.[9]

Facilitation is an informal process in which a third party which is powerless to impose solutions on the disputants helps them craft an acceptable settlement. Facilitation has the transformative potential to encourage moral growth in people by helping them—in the very midst of conflict—to wrestle with difficult inner and outer circumstances and bridge human differences.[10]

[7] Ibid., p. 41.

[8] A. Smith, 'Commonwealth Cross Sections: Prenegotiation to Minimize Conflict and Develop Cooperation', in A. Lall (ed.), *Multilateral Negotiation and Mediation: Instruments and Methods*, New York: Pergamon and the International Peace Academy, 1985, pp. 53–73.

[9] Mark Hoffmann, 'Third Party Mediation and Conflict Resolution in the Post-Cold War Era', in John Baylis and N. J. Rengger (eds.), *Dilemmas of World Politics: International Issues in a Changing World*, Oxford: Clarendon, 1992, p. 172.

[10] Robert A. Bush and Joseph P. Folger, *The Promise of Mediation: Responding to Conflict through Empowerment and Recognition*, San Francisco: Jossey-Bass, 1994.

Facilitation is similar to conciliation. It is informal, non-coercive and non-hierarchical in character. It is a pre-negotiation activity in which the third party does not directly participate in or influence negotiations between parties. Instead, the facilitator helps prepare such an environment and conditions where bilateral negotiations can be fruitful. The facilitators are not expected to offer their own ideas for solving the conflict, but guide the participants in processes such as problem solving, prioritizing, and planning. They help the parties to keep the negotiations on track, and work towards mutually advantageous outcomes. Norway's intervention to get Israel and the PLO make the Oslo Declaration of Principles on Interim Self-government Arrangements in September 1993 is a good example of facilitation. Most present-day peace processes also fall in this category of third-party activities.

Mediation

The concept and functions of mediation are discussed in the ensuing section.

THE CONCEPT AND HISTORY OF INTERNATIONAL MEDIATION

The theory and practice of mediation are derived from several disciplinary sources: psychology, sociology, anthropology, political science, international relations, communication and management studies. For long, systematic and conceptual studies on international mediation were not available as the practitioners of mediation 'were keen to sustain its perception as a mysterious practice taking place behind closed doors, and scholars of mediation did not think it was susceptible to a systematic analysis'.[11] However, the post-World War II period witnessed extensive engagement of academics in empirical and theoretical studies that shed light on the concept, nature, stages and effectiveness of international mediation.

[11] Jacob Bercovitch, 'The Structure and Diversity of Mediation in International Relations', in Jacob Bercovitch and Jeffrey Rubin (eds.), *Mediation in International Relations*, New York: St. Martin's Press, 1992, p. 2.

DEFINITIONS OF MEDIATION

Defining mediation is not simple. Various definitions are offered by scholars, causing confusion and contradictions in the literature on the subject. International mediation is a dynamic, diverse, multi-faceted and complex activity which can be carried out in formal or informal manner, openly or secretly. It can assume several forms depending upon the conditions, parties involved, contextual factors, and attributes of the mediator. Hence, different meanings have been attributed to mediation. Not just the meanings, even the objectives of mediation are interpreted differently. Moreover, as theorizing on mediation is largely practice-driven, its understanding and definitions have been evolving and altering with changes in its practice. The term is often used in a confusing, imprecise and generic sense to indicate any third-party activity short of armed intervention.[12] Some scholars regard conciliation and facilitation as types of mediation. It is, therefore, essential to clarify the meaning of international mediation and identify its parameters.

Listed below are some definitions of mediation:

1. Mediation involves the intervention of a skilled and experienced intermediary who attempts to facilitate a negotiated settlement of the substantive issues that comprise the dispute.... The traditional form of *pure mediation* in which the third party has no power over the outcome can be distinguished from *power mediation*...in which a powerful third party uses coercion or 'leverage'... in the form of promised rewards or threatened punishments to motivate the parties toward a settlement.[13]
2. Mediation involves the intervention of a third party, which first investigates and defines the problem, and then usually approaches each group separately with recommendations designed to provide a mutually acceptable solution.[14]

[12] Burton and Dukes, *Conflict: Practices in Management*, p. 25.

[13] Fisher, *Beyond Confrantation*, p. 41.

[14] Robert R. Blake and Jane Srygley Mouton, *Solving Costly Organizational Conflicts*, San Francisco: Jossey-Bass, 1985, p. 15.

3. Mediation is a process by which an impartial third person (sometimes more than one person) helps parties to resolve disputes through mutual concessions and face-to-face bargaining.[15]
4. Mediation is 'a process of conflict management, related to but distinct from the parties' own efforts, where the disputing parties or their representatives seek the assistance, or accept an offer of help, from an individual, group, state or organization to change, affect or influence their perceptions or behavior, without resorting to physical force or invoking the authority of the law'.[16]
5. Mediation is quintessentially a method of mitigating concerns through the presence and support of an intermediary who is not party to the conflict, who enjoys the trust of the disputants, and whose goal is to help the disputants forge agreements which they find acceptable. By virtue of these characteristics, the intermediary serves as both a buffer and a bridge between the antagonists, ameliorating the anger and suspicion that prevent them from addressing, in a cooperative manner, the substantive issues in dispute. The parties' common trust in the mediator offsets their mutual distrust and raises their confidence in negotiations. This is the basic logic and potential of mediation.[17]

This study has conceived of mediation as a process in which the conflicting parties seek the assistance of, or accept an offer of help from an outside individual, organization or state to be able to manage their conflict peacefully and/or prevent critical deterioration in their relationship. Such intervention by the outside party is non-coercive and non-binding. Mediation is a dynamic

[15] Robert Coulson, *Fighting Fair: Family Mediation Will Work for You*, New York: Free Press, 1983.

[16] Bercovitch, 'Structure and Diversity of Mediation', p. 8.

[17] Laurie Nathan, 'When Push Comes to Shove: The Failure of International Mediation in African Civil Wars', *Track II*: http://ccrweb.ccr.uct.ac.za/two/8_2/vol8no2.html, November 1999.

activity in which conciliation and facilitation also form different components and phases of the triadic process of peacemaking. In the facilitative and transformative form of mediation, the mediator aims at altering underlying conditions of the conflict, channelling information to the involved parties and facilitating cooperation between them, but not intervening in the formal process or substance of mediation.

History of Mediation

Third-party mediation has been applied since the beginning of society in all informal and formal group processes. Even when there is a conflict among the members of a family, friends or well-wishers help to moderate relations among them. Individuals, groups and states have turned to external actors whenever they have been unable to manage or settle disputes on their own. Mediation has been practised both in Eastern and Western societies. References to mediation are found in the Bible and in Homer's *Iliad*.[18] Records of mediation in community disputes in early Chinese and African societies are also available.[19] The Indian epic *Mahabharata*, written about five thousand years ago, depicts Lord Krishna acting as a mediator to avoid a war between the Pandavas and the Kauravas. Similarly, Arab-Islamic traditions also have precedents of conflict management through third-party mediation. Techniques, procedures and rituals such as *wasta* (patronage-mediation), *tahkeem* (arbitration), *sulh* (settlement), and *musalaha* (reconciliation) are examples of modes of mediation in the Arab-Islamic cultural traditions.[20] Christian groups like the Quakers, Mennonites and the Brethren have been prominent in practising mediation as a method of conflict resolution.

[18] Bercovitch, *Mediation in International Relations*, p. 1.

[19] Burton and Dukes, *Conflict: Practices in Management*, p. 26.

[20] George E. Irani, 'Islamic Mediation Techniques for Middle East Conflicts', *Middle East Review of International Affairs*, vol. 3, no. 2, June 1999, p. 2.

Mediation in the Domestic Context

Mediation on a large scale and in a formal manner began with the labour-management disputes in the US. It has also been used extensively for the settlement of consumer disputes, divorce and child custody cases, and neighbourhood, inter-corporate, school or environmental disputes. In many of these mediation efforts, volunteers as well as professional and trained mediators participate as negotiators and conciliators. Mediation has now emerged as an important method of dispute settlement providing an alternative to expensive and prolonged procedures of courts and tribunals. A number of public agencies in the US like the Federal Mediation and Conciliation Service (FMCS) under the Department of Labor, and the Community Relations Service (CRS) have promoted mediation as a technique of alternative dispute resolution. Most of the states in the US have some statutory authority for mediation. Mediation has also been institutionalized in several European and Asian countries.

Mediation in the International System

Formal mediation at the international level has a comparatively short history. The Declaration of Paris (1856) expressed the hope that the signatories would seek mediation for settling their disputes. At the Second Hague Conference (1907), the right of the states to mediate was acknowledged. The US served as mediator between Bolivia and Chile in 1882 during the War of the Pacific (1879–84) over Chile's possession of the Bolivian port of Antofagasta and the province of Atacama. American President Theodore Roosevelt also performed a mediatory role in the Russo–Japanese war (1904–5) and brought the two parties to an agreement after talks at Portsmouth, in the summer of 1905. The Second Hague Conference recognized the right of the states to offer mediation to their friends. The Covenant of the League of Nations offered the services of the League for conciliation between states. The Charter of the United Nations also calls for submitting disputes to mediation on the recommendation of the

Security Council. The UN has mediated several conflicts in the last five decades. Regional organizations like the Organization of American States (OAS) and the Organization of African Unity (OAU) have also functioned as mediators.

The Middle East conflict is probably the most mediated conflict in recent times. It has invited intensive and high-profile involvement of the US. Confidence building measures like demilitarized zones, interposition of international observer forces, direct communications, and joint consultative commissions to resolve disputes over the interpretation of data between Israel and Egypt after the 1973 Arab–Israeli war became possible due to American involvement. The Camp David Accord signed between Egypt and Israel in September 1978 has been celebrated as one of the biggest successes of American mediation. With the assistance of US President Jimmy Carter and after 12 days of secret negotiations at Camp David, Egyptian President Anwar Sadat and Israeli Prime Minister Menachem Begin signed two agreements at the White House. These agreements defined the future relations between the two adversaries, and contained provisions regarding the withdrawal of Israeli forces from the Sinai province of Egypt, military arrangements in the peninsula such as demilitarization and limitations, as well as the supervision mechanism. However, the agreement was uncertain regarding the future of the Palestinian areas of the West Bank and Gaza.[21]

After the Gulf War of 1990, the US and other Western states displayed keen interest in initiating a peace process in the Middle East. A peace conference between Israel and the PLO was held in Madrid in 1990. A breakthrough was achieved in the form of autonomy agreements signed between Israel and the PLO in 1993, followed by another agreement in 1995. The peace accord between Jordan and Israel in 1994, and the Wye River Accord of 1998 also became possible due to the significant role of external actors in the Middle East peace process.

[21] David W. Lesch, *1979: The Year that Defined the Modern Middle East*, Boulder: Westview Press, 2001.

There have also been several other major attempts at international mediation in recent history. Algeria acted as a go-between in securing the release of American citizens held hostage by Iran in the early 1980s. The Geneva Accords that brought the conflict in Afghanistan between the militant mujahideen groups and the Soviet-supported government in Kabul to an end was mediated by the UN. The UN mediation was instrumental in bringing South Africa, Cuba and Angola to an agreement over the issue of complete independence for the south-western African colony of Namibia. The agreement among the three parties was signed at the UN headquarters in December 1988, paving the way for the independence of Namibia and implementation of the Security Council Resolution 435 in this regard. The UN also mediated and supervised the end of Vietnam's military occupation of Cambodia and the transition of Cambodia from communism to a liberal democratic system in the late 1980s and early 1990s. The UN, the US and the European Union attempted to mediate the ethnic conflict between and within the former provinces of Yugoslavia, viz., Bosnia and Herzegovina. The US also brokered the agreement on Northern Ireland in 1998. The experience of the post-World War II period reveals that most mediation efforts were carried out by the Western states, while most conflicts in which mediation was applied occurred in the developing world.[22]

THE ROLE OF INTERNATIONAL MEDIATION

Mediation is the continuation of the parties' own efforts to settle their differences through negotiations and mutual concessions. A mediator rarely performs a single, set role. The traditional image of a mediator does not fully capture the intricacies of a mediator's job, as:

[22] Moonis Ahmar, 'Gains and Costs of Third Party Mediation: A Case Study of India-Pakistan Normalization Process', unpublished paper submitted at the international conference on Cooperation in South Asia: Resolution of Interstate Conflicts, South Asian Studies Division, School of International Studies, Jawaharlal Nehru University, New Delhi, 29–30 March 1999, p. 3.

a single, usually prestigious figure traveling between capital and capital with a briefcase full of peace plans, compromise solutions and face-saving formulae, ready to produce these as soon as he confronts the leaders of the parties in conflict and hoping that, by use of ingenious arguments and the force of his prestige, one or other of his schemes will provide the long-sought-for solution.[23]

A mediator can be an observer, communicator, adviser, facilitator, conciliator, enunciator, prompter, advocate, leader, negotiator, manipulator, solution-seeker and solution-giver. He executes these varying functions depending upon the nature and the stage of an international conflict. I. William Zartman and Saadia Touval categorize basic mediator roles as communicator, formulator, and manipulator.[24]

The elemental task of a mediator is to act as a catalyst and a communication channel and help the parties develop alternative proposals for the settlement of their dispute. A mediator creates the right setting and mood in which the parties can carry out negotiations in an agreeable style. During negotiations, the mediator can assist the parties to set the terms and limits of their bargaining and formulate options for the settlement of their conflict. It may also have to act as a moderator or a referee to see that negotiation schedules are maintained and commitments made by the parties are fulfilled.

Edward de Bono describes the role of a third party thus:

From the detached and superior viewpoint, the third party is in the best position to see the whole map. As a result the third party can make connections and can show how one matter connects up with another. The third party can also show two things which might appear different really have much in common. The third party can also show how under certain circumstances different aims can be reconciled. The third party

[23] C.R. Mitchell, *Structure of International Conflict*, London: Macmillan, 1981, p. 287.

[24] I. William Zartman and Saadia Touval, 'International Mediation: Conflict Resolution and Power Politics', *Journal of Social Issues*, vol. 41, no. 2, pp. 27–45, 1985.

can make bridges. The third party can drop in a connector which suddenly brings about an insight switch of perception.[25]

An accomplished mediator takes into consideration not just the expressed or explicit interests of the parties, but also their unexpressed and covert interests. Due to persuasion of the mediator, the parties can discover common interests and move towards the resolution of their conflict, building upon these common interests. A problem-solving and consensus-building approach is the key to success of international mediation. This approach has to be applied right from the initiation of a mediation process during which the mediator attempts to alter the prevalent mistrust and misperceptions among adversaries and convert a win-lose conflict situation into a win-win one. Although a mediator can play several kinds of roles in a theoretical sense, according to a study by Jacob Bercovitch, a mediator's functions in reality are fairly restricted and elementary. According to Bercovitch's findings, in about 49 per cent of cases of international mediation between 1945 and 1995, the mediator's role was confined to communication and facilitation, rather than extending to procedure and substance of negotiations.[26]

Mediation can be of two kinds: agreement-centred and relationship-centred. The first form concentrates on reaching an agreement acceptable to both parties as the final outcome. It relies on bargaining, and alerts the parties to the dangers of continuing the conflict. On the other hand, rather than producing an agreement right away, relationship-centred mediation addresses the imperative of improving the relationship between adversaries and the environment in which their relationship functions.[27] Though these two approaches are not mutually exclusive, their emphasis, normative assumptions and orientations are dissimilar.

[25] Edward de Bono, *Conflicts: A Better Way to Resolve Them*, London: Penguin, 1991, p. 131.

[26] Jacob Bercovitch and Allison Houston, 'Why Do They Do It Like This? An Analysis of the Factors Influencing Mediation Behavior in International Conflicts', *Journal of Conflict Resolution*, vol. 44, no. 2, April 2000, p. 185.

[27] Burton and Dukes, *Conflict: Practices in Management*, p. 32.

THE MEDIATION PROCESS

Conditions for the Initiation and Success of Mediation

In most cases, mediation is initiated after the conflict has become prolonged and complex and the conflicting parties have exhausted all options of settlement through their own efforts. For the initiation and success of a mediation effort, the following conditions are required:

1. Realization by the parties that they cannot settle their differences through bilateral negotiations because their negotiations have reached a deadlock.
2. Realization by the parties that they cannot get what they want through unilateral action.
3. Willingness of the disputant parties to undertake mediation for the peaceful management and resolution of their conflict.
4. Suitability of the issues of the conflict to international mediation.
5. Willingness of the mediator to get involved in the conflict.
6. Credibility and acceptance of the mediator by the parties.
7. Leverage enjoyed by the mediator over the disputant parties.
8. Mediating ability, knowledge and skills of the mediator.
9. Support of the key internal political constituencies for mediation.
10. Support of the major international systemic actors for a mediated settlement.

Stages of Mediation

As stated earlier, mediation is not so much a *technique* as a *process* of resolving conflicts. It is not a one-time action, but a series of actions. Moore has given a comprehensive division of the process of mediation into 12 stages:[28]

[28] See Christopher W. Moore, *The Mediation Process: Practical Strategies for Resolving Conflict*, San Francisco: Jossey-Bass, 1987.

1. Initial contact with the disputing parties.
2. Selecting a strategy to guide mediation.
3. Collecting and analysing background information.
4. Designing a detailed plan for mediation.
5. Building trust and cooperation.
6. Beginning the mediation session.
7. Defining issues and setting agenda.
8. Uncovering hidden interests of the disputing parties.
9. Generating options for settlement.
10. Assessing options for settlement.
11. Final bargaining.
12. Achieving formal settlement.

Variables Influencing the Mediation Process

International mediation is a complex and diverse process that operates at several levels. The applicability and success of mediation depend upon a multiplicity of variables and contextual factors: the nature of the dispute, of the parties and of the mediators; pre-existing context of the conflict; environmental and systemic variables; timing of the mediation initiative; capabilities of the parties and the mediator; interests of the adversaries and the mediator; previous relations between the parties and the mediator; skills, knowledge and previous record of the mediator; activities of other international actors.

Jacob Bercovitch has presented what he calls a contingency model of mediation that conceives international mediation and its outcomes as contingent upon various contextual and process variables. Contextual variables are constituted of the nature of the parties, nature of the dispute, and the nature of the mediator. The process variables are constituted of the nature of the mediation activities. Together, both these variables determine the outcomes of the mediation effort.[29]

Mediation and Power

Power dynamics are central to all third-party activity. Mediation is carried out within the framework of control and influence. The

[29] Bercovitch and Houston, 'Why Do They Do It Like This', pp. 185–90.

distribution of power between the two parties and between the mediator and the parties shapes the process and outcomes of international mediation. The leverage and the resources that a mediator possesses and the kind of incentives and disincentives it offers to the parties will determine the effectiveness of mediation. Such 'leverage or resources buttress the mediator's ability to facilitate a successful outcome through the balancing of power discrepancies and enhancing of co-operative behaviour'.[30] Often, when the disputing nations are weak and small and the mediator is a very powerful state, mediation actually becomes a one-way process of imposition of the will of the mediator on the parties. The Soviet mediation between the East European states during the Cold War era, or America's mediation in the conflicts among the Latin American states is an illustration of such a process.

The employment of power and coercion converts the mediator from a communicator into the mediator as a manipulator, wherein: 'the mediator uses its power to bring the parties to an agreement, pushing and pulling them away from conflict and into resolution. ... The mediator may have to go so far as to improve the absolute attractiveness of the resolution by increasing the unattractiveness of continued conflict, which may mean shoring up one side or condemning another.'[31]

Interests of the Mediator

Most mediators choose to mediate out of self-interest rather than altruism. Instances of genuinely humanitarian mediation are few. The involvement of external actors and their willingness to mediate are directly proportionate to their interests—economic, political, or strategic. The third party, in this sense, is not a disin-

[30] I. William Zartman and Saadia Touval, 'Mediation: The Role of Third-Party Diplomacy and Informal Peacemaking', in S. J. Brown and K.M. Schraub (eds.), *Resolving Third World Conflict: Challenges for a New Era,* Washington: The United States Institute for Peace, 1992, p. 253.

[31] Jacob Bercovitch and Allison Houston, 'The Study of International Mediation: Theoretical Issues and Empirical Evidence', in Jacob Bercovitch (ed.), *Resolving International Conflicts: The Theory and Practice of Mediation,* Boulder and London: Lynne Rienner, 1996, p. 26.

terested, detached outsider, but indirectly a participant in the conflict trying to take it in a particular direction desired by it. A mediator can have two kinds of interests in mediation: defensive and offensive. If the continuation of a conflict threatens the mediator's own interests, it makes a defensive intervention to safeguard its own position. Also, if a conflict is between two allies of the mediator, or if a conflict threatens to upset the regional balance of power, or if the conflict is likely to escalate to a stage where weapons causing enormous damage might be used, international mediation may be undertaken for a defensive purpose. The second motive of a mediator can be offensive, i.e. its desire to expand its sphere of influence in the region where the conflict is taking place, or reduce the opponent's influence over the parties.

Neutrality of the Mediator

Almost everyone thinks that the mediator ought to be neutral and impartial between the parties, that it should not have any agenda and interests of its own while pursuing mediation. It is true that a thoroughly biased mediator who is aligned with one party cannot carry out genuine intermediary activity, and that the mediator is expected to treat the parties with a certain degree of evenhandedness. The mediator should also avoid taking public positions on the outcome of the conflict, or comment on which party should take how much blame for the continuation of the conflict. However, the expectation of complete mediator neutrality is not justified by empirical realities. The celebrated neutrality of a mediator is more notional than real. It is impossible that while mediating a mediator would be completely free from biases and prejudices, or that it would be indifferent to its own short-term and long-term interests. The mediating persons' personal, national and cultural biases and values are bound to influence their preferences on what constitutes a just and equitable solution to the dispute, and what kind of regional order is desirable. Hence, what can be minimally expected of a mediator is evenhandedness in the treatment of the two parties, rather than denial of its own national background and choices.

Secrecy and the Mediation Process

Secret diplomacy is not regarded as a good practice. However, international mediation is sometimes carried out secretly. Secrecy helps avoid the negative influence of such forces that are opposed to the conflict resolution process and regard negotiations with the adversary as a sign of weakness. If the mediated negotiations are to succeed:

> [T]hey must be shrouded in a veil of secrecy. If all the twists and turns of negotiations are made public, then the lobbies and vested interests of both parties get activated, creating more and more roadblocks, which then become impossible to surmount.... Media hype distorts reality, provides entertainment, complicates issues, intensifies pressures and eventually guarantees both fatigue and failure.[32]

The parties involved in the mediation process may issue public denial of such an effort during the pre-negotiation phase up to the time an agreement is reached about launching the formal and advanced phase of mediation. Secret mediation made Egyptian President Anwar Sadat's visit to Israel possible in 1977. Secret parleys in the presence of American, Canadian and European mediators in Oslo in 1993 were an important factor in finalizing the agreements between Israel and the PLO.

The Skills of the Mediator

The consequences of mediation are determined a great deal by the skills and commitment of the mediator and its ability to cut through deadlock in negotiations. The mediating persons need to have several personal and diplomatic skills to succeed in their task. Apart from deep knowledge of the problems and issues of the conflict, the mediator should have familiarity with the peace processes in different regions and the role of mediation in them. He should also possess excellent communication abilities, credibility, skills in crisis management, and the ability to listen patiently to and sympathize with the parties. A mediator working in

[32] Anita Pratap, 'A Neo-Realist Script', *Outlook*: http://www.outlookindia.com/full.asp?fodname=20010806&fname=Column+Anita+%28F%29&sid=1, 6 August 2001

a cross-cultural situation should also be sensitive to the cultural and social characteristics of the parties.

MEDIATOR CATEGORIES

The range of actors who can mediate in international conflicts is really large, considering the proliferation of the state and non-state actors in the present international system. For the sake of convenience, the actors who can mediate in interstate disputes can be divided into three categories: states; international and regional organizations; and private individuals, groups and organizations. Moreover, since mediation is a multi-level activity, co-mediation by these actors simultaneously is also possible, depending upon the type of international conflict.

STATES

Because the most violent and pervasive conflicts occur between states, it is natural that other states act as mediators more often than other actors. Despite the proliferation of multitudes of non-state actors, the state is still the most powerful and decisive actor in the international system. Moreover, in comparison to other actors, mediation by states is regarded as accountable in some sense to the people and to the international organizations of which they are members. When a state mediates, it nominates one person, or a group of persons (who could be officials, members of the cabinet, scholars, or any other category of individuals) skilled in mediation procedures to represent it. These mediators carry authority from their governments to move the mediation in the desired direction and continually report back to them on the progress of mediation. Differences between states in their size, power, resources, geographic location and cultural background impinge on their willingness and capacity to mediate.

INTERNATIONAL ORGANIZATIONS

The post-World War II period has been marked by a remarkable growth in the number and type of international and regional organizations. Normally, the organization of which both the disputant parties are members acts as a mediating agency. However, even other international organizations with sufficient leverage can lend a helping hand to solve the conflict. The UN, of course, has been the most accepted and active international organization for mediation between states. It has intervened in a large number of interstate disputes to achieve ceasefire or settlement of disputes. Regional organizations like the Organization of African Unity (OAU), Organization of American States (OAS) and the Arab League have also functioned as mediators in conflicts between their members.

Private Individuals and Organizations

International mediation can also be carried out by private individuals and non-governmental organizations. Individuals of repute (former statesmen, retired diplomats, scholars and so on) have been recognized as private intermediaries in conflicts. Dag Hammarskjöld, U. Thant, Henry Kissinger, Terry Waite, Jimmy Carter, Desmond Tutu and Nelson Mandela have played mediatory roles in their official as well as non-official capacities. Of course, the legitimacy and the power of the organizations or the states they belonged to contributed to their effectiveness as mediators. The Quakers, the World Council of Churches, the International Committee of the Red Cross and the Society of Friends have also been prominent non-official organizations acting as mediators in international conflicts. In comparison to states or international organizations, mediation by private individuals and groups tends to be more flexible and less coercive.

CHAPTER 3

History of International Mediation in India–Pakistan Conflict

The India–Pakistan conflict has seen formal and informal intervention by external actors since its inception. Discussed below are the significant cases of third-party role organized chronologically.

MEDIATION BY THE UNITED NATIONS (1948–65)

The India–Pakistan conflict and the Kashmir dispute formed one of the earliest instances of mediation by the United Nations. The involvement of the UN in the Kashmir dispute began with the complaint lodged by India under Art. 35 of the UN Charter to the president of the Security Council on 1 January 1948 against Pakistan for its alleged military, logistical and monetary support to the invasion of Jammu & Kashmir by tribal infiltrators. India urged the Security Council to prevent Pakistan's government from aiding and participating in the invasion of an area which was legally and constitutionally a part of India, and take appropriate action to restore peace. On the basis of this complaint, along with a parallel request from Pakistan to look at the legality of the accession of the princely states of Jammu & Kashmir, Junagadh, and Hyderabad to India, the UN Commission on India and Pakistan (UNCIP) was set up in June 1948 under the chairmanship of Joseph Corbel from Czechoslovakia. Other countries represented on the commission were the United States, Argentina, Colombia, and Belgium.

The US, which was the most influential power in the UN at that time, also favoured to the idea of the global body getting involved in the Kashmir dispute. A position paper prepared for the American delegation to the UN General Assembly in 1947 stated that the US would much prefer that the Kashmir question be settled by direct negotiations between India and Pakistan. But given the existing conditions, it felt it needed external assistance to manage the conflict in South Asia. As 'the British are apparently not in a position to render this outside assistance, and rather than have the role fall either to the United States or any other single third party, assumption by the United Nations of the problem would be preferred'.[1]

The UNCIP was assigned the task of visiting the subcontinent and holding discussions with the leadership of India and Pakistan in order to help bring the war to an end. After ceasefire and fulfillment of the conditions specified in the UN resolution, a plebiscite was to be held under an impartial administration to ascertain the wishes of the people of Jammu & Kashmir on their future status. India and Pakistan agreed to the proposal of the UNCIP to constitute a special three-member Commission on Mediation which would visit Kashmir to investigate facts and hold dialogue with the two governments on the issue. Subsequent to the ceasefire agreement between India and Pakistan in July 1949 at Karachi, the establishment of the UN Military Observers' Group in India and Pakistan (UNMOGIP) was also authorized. This group, consisting of multinational military personnel, carried the responsibility of monitoring the observance of ceasefire and reporting to each party and to the UN Secretary-General on violations of the Ceasefire Line (CFL) or on any activity along the CFL that was detrimental to the maintenance of stability and peace.

After visiting India and Pakistan and meetings with policy makers, the UNCIP submitted several proposals for the demilitarization of the state, as well as a proposal for settling the dispute through arbitration. However, these proposals were not wholly acceptable to India and Pakistan. It is not pertinent to recount here the details of the various interim reports submitted by the

[1] Cited by Manoj Joshi, *The Lost Rebellion: Kashmir in the Nineties*, New Delhi: Penguin Books, 1999, p. 297.

UNCIP to the Security Council from 1948 to 1949, except the acknowledgement made, with a sense of resignation and frustration, by the commission in its third interim report, to the Security Council on 5 December 1949, that it would have a limited role in brokering an agreement between India and Pakistan as 'the situation in the State has changed, the [Security Council] resolutions remain unchanged'.[2]

The commission then suggested that a single mediator be appointed for the Kashmir problem. Canadian Gen. McNaughton, the then president of the Security Council, was named the mediator by the UNCIP. He could not make any progress in the resolution of the vexed problem. His position that Pakistan and Kashmir were equal parties in the dispute along with India was totally unacceptable to the Indian government. In April 1950, the Security Council decided to convert the UNCIP into a one-member UN Representative on India and Pakistan. Owen Dixon, an Australian jurist, was appointed the UN Representative. He was authorized to explore all alternatives and offer suggestions to expedite the solution of the Kashmir dispute. He suggested two plans for the resolution of the Kashmir dispute. These plans envisaged a partition of the state between India and Pakistan on the basis of a plebiscite. The first plan proposed separate area-wise plebiscite in the whole of Kashmir. Each area would then join India or Pakistan depending on the outcome of the voting. The second plan suggested allocating parts of Kashmir to India or Pakistan on the basis of their known preferences without holding a plebiscite. A plebiscite would be held only in those parts where both India and Pakistan claimed support. Not surprisingly, his proposals were also a non-starter. In April 1951, Dixon was replaced by Frank P. Graham, who had been a member of the American Senate and of the UN Commission on Indonesia. Even his proposal, first for the demilitarization of Jammu & Kashmir, and later for arbitration of the dispute, failed to elicit a positive response from the two governments.

[2] Quoted by A. Appadorai and M.S. Rajan, *India's Foreign Policy and Relations*, New Delhi: South Asian Publishers, 1985, p. 85.

Interestingly, both Dixon and Graham, realizing the futility of persisting with UN mediation and international involvement in finding a solution to the Kashmir problem, suggested that direct negotiation between India and Pakistan was the best available choice. The last report submitted by Graham to the Security Council clearly stated that the issue should be passed on to the two governments to settle between themselves. Graham wrote in his report:

> Instead of the United Nations' representative continuing to report differences to the Security Council, may the leadership of over 400,000,000 people, with the goodwill and assistance of the United Nations, join in negotiating and reporting an agreement on Kashmir and thereby light a torch along the difficult path of the people's pilgrimage to peace.[3]

Graham's suggestion was accepted by the Security Council, and direct negotiations were held between India and Pakistan from 1953 to 1956. During this period, the Security Council did not get involved with the Kashmir question. Upon Pakistan's request that as the direct negotiations had failed the Security Council should ask India to honour its commitments made to the UN, the council again took up the matter from January 1957. Malik Firoz Khan Noon from Pakistan and V.K. Krishna Menon from India presented the cases of their respective states at the UN in a spirited manner. The members of the Security Council seemed to agree with Noon more than with Krishna Menon. A resolution was introduced in the council asking for a UN force in Kashmir prior to withdrawal of the Indian and Pakistani forces. This resolution was vetoed by the Soviet Union.

Subsequently, the president of the Security Council and the representative of Sweden, Gunnar Jarring, was asked to re-examine proposals for the settlement of the Kashmir dispute and discuss them with the governments of India and Pakistan. Jarring did not succeed in his task. However, in his report, he noted that implementation of the original Security Council resolutions may be rendered more difficult with the changing international and

[3] Ibid., p. 86.

regional situation. After debating on Jarring's report, the Security Council requested the UN Representative Frank P. Graham to make recommendations for the implementation of the resolutions of the UNCIP of 1948 and 1949 on demilitarization of the area, administration of the region under the surveillance of the UNCIP (and its successor UN Representative for India and Pakistan), and holding of plebiscite. Graham found several drawbacks in these resolutions with regard to clarification of the modalities of the withdrawal of Pakistani troops from the area; the question of the sovereignty over Jammu & Kashmir during the period of surveillance by the UN; ambiguity regarding terms like surveillance and local authority, etc. Keeping these problems in view, Graham negotiated with the representatives of India and Pakistan, and made recommendations to create and maintain an atmosphere conducive to the implementation of the UN resolutions. Even as Pakistan accepted these recommendations made in April 1958, India rejected them because, in the words of Jawaharlal Nehru, 'any consideration...which endeavours to put us on the same level as Pakistan—that is, the aggressor and the aggressed countries on the same level—is not agreeable to us and will not be accepted by us'.[4] Effectively, the Indian response signified the end of the UN role in Kashmir. Pakistan, however, continued to refer the issue to the Security Council, which discussed Kashmir in its meetings in February, April and June 1962 and in February and May 1964 without any concrete progress. The UN finally came to realize the weight of the suggestion made by Owen Dixon in 1950 and reaffirmed by Frank Graham in 1953 that the issue was best left for the two states to manage and resolve through direct negotiations. All through the period of the mediation by the UN, the US and the UK exercised controlling influence over the decisions of the Security Council.

The subsequent UN involvement in the India–Pakistan conflict was confined to pressing for ceasefire after the 1965 and 1971 wars and making regular, platitudinous appeals for peaceful

[4] Prime Minister Jawaharlal Nehru's statement at a press conference on 4 April 1958, quoted in Appadorai and Rajan, *India's Foreign Policy*, p. 92.

resolution of the conflict. This involvement has not been mediatory in nature. U Thant, Secretary-General of the UN, visited India and Pakistan in early September 1965 during the war to press for ceasefire and reconciliation. After the end of the war in September 1965, the UN India Pakistan Observers Mission (UNIPOM) was constituted for a brief period to monitor the withdrawal of the troops to their original positions on the CFL.

The UNMOGIP has, however, continued its activities after the 1965 and 1971 wars. The 1971 war changed a number of positions on both sides of the 1949 CFL. In July 1972, India and Pakistan signed an agreement defining the Line of Control (LOC) in Kashmir which followed the same course as the CFL established by the Karachi Agreement in 1949, with minor modifications. India took the position that the mandate of the UNMOGIP had lapsed, since it related specifically to the CFL under the Karachi Agreement. Pakistan, however, did not accept this position. Given the disagreement between the two parties about the UNMOGIP's mandate and functions, the Secretary General's position has been that the UNMOGIP could be terminated only by a decision of the Security Council. The military authorities of Pakistan have continued to lodge complaints with the UNMOGIP about ceasefire violations. The military authorities of India have lodged no complaints since January 1972, and have restricted the activities of the UN observers on the Indian side of the LOC. They have, however, continued to provide accommodation, transport and other facilities to the UNMOGIP. The group, operating from India for six months (May to October), and from Pakistan for the other six months (November to April), today consists of about 44 military observers and an equal number of civilian staff.

India has taken a consistent stand against any sort of UN mediation or involvement in the Kashmir dispute since the late 1960s. In 1993, when UN Secretary General Boutros Boutros Ghali made an offer to India's Minister of External Affairs Dinesh Singh for provision of any UN assistance to settle the problems it created a storm in a teacup over the likely revival of UN mediation on Kashmir. India firmly and flatly rejected Ghali's offer of 'assistance'. For Pakistan, mediation by the UN may be an ongoing and live affair, but it is able to secure little support among other countries or in the UN itself about its demand to get the UN resolution on plebiscite in Jammu & Kashmir implemented.

MEDIATION IN THE INDUS WATER DISPUTE (1952–60)

The treaty on the sharing of the Indus River water—the most significant economic cooperation agreement between India and Pakistan—signed in 1960 is an instance of successful mediation in an India–Pakistan dispute. Despite three wars and unrelenting strains in the relations of the two countries, this treaty has survived. After Partition of the subcontinent in 1947, the distribution of waters of the rivers flowing from Jammu & Kashmir into Pakistan's territory became a contentious issue. The Standstill Agreement for continuing with the pre-Partition allocation of water in the Indus river irrigation system expired on 1 April 1948, after which the East Punjab government on the Indian side cut-off water supply from the Upper Bari Doab Canal to the Central Bari Doab Canal in Pakistan because the water dues had not been paid by Pakistan. This action threatened the agricultural sector in Pakistan, and caused steep deterioration in bilateral relations. India felt that Partition had left India at a disadvantage in terms of irrigation in Punjab because, of the total land of undivided Punjab, Pakistan received 18 million field acres of irrigated land, while India received only 5 million field acres of irrigated land. Pakistan, on its part, felt that its agricultural and food security was threatened in the absence of a guarantee of steady supply of water from the Indian side. As the conflict in Kashmir became more intense, and as India announced plans for the construction of dams on the rivers of the Indus basin, emotions in Pakistan ran high.

In February 1951, David Lilienthal, former chairman of the Tennessee Valley Authority and the US Atomic Energy Commission, visited India and Pakistan to write a series of articles on India–Pakistan relations for *Collier's* magazine. He met top leaders like Jawaharlal Nehru and Liaquat Ali Khan for this purpose.

Before coming to the subcontinent, he had meetings with influential Americans like Secretary of State Dean Acheson, and scholar and journalist Walter Lippman. In his articles, he suggested that India and Pakistan work out a programme for joint development and operation of the Indus basin river system, upon which both nations were dependent for irrigation water. With more dams and irrigation canals, the Indus and its tributaries could be made to yield additional water needed for increased food production. He also suggested that the World Bank could act as a mediator for reaching such an agreement, and also finance the Indus basin development projects.

President of the World Bank Eugene R. Black favoured this suggestion. The original proposal of the World Bank in 1952 offering its good offices and comprehensive support for the development of the Indus basin was rejected by India. However, the experts nominated by the World Bank put forward another set of proposals in 1954. The crux of these proposals was that the waters of the three eastern rivers (Ravi, Beas, and Sutlej) should be used exclusively by India, while those of the three western rivers (Indus, Jhelum, and Chenab) should be utilized by Pakistan, except for a small volume to be used in Kashmir. A new set of canals and storage reservoirs should be constructed to help Pakistan receive the irrigation water from the western rivers. India and Pakistan were receptive to the proposals. After a series of meetings among engineers and experts of the two countries in Washington, Rome and London, the Indus Water Treaty was finalized and signed by Indian Prime Minister Jawaharlal Nehru, Pakistani President Ayub Khan, and Vice-President of the World Bank W.A.B. Illif at Karachi in 1960.

The treaty incorporated most of the proposals of the World Bank. India was also permitted non-consumptive use of the western rivers flowing into Pakistan. It provided for arbitration to settle future disputes and set up the permanent Indus Commission to facilitate regular communication and control over the distribution of water. The treaty created a fund for the development of the Indus basin in which the World Bank and the governments of the US, Canada, UK, West Germany, Australia and New Zealand agreed to contribute about $1 billion to finance the construction of large storage dams and other hydrological development works to be undertaken by Pakistan. It is beyond doubt that the Indus Water Treaty would not have been possible without the mediation of the World Bank. Both Nehru and Ayub Khan paid rich tributes to the World Bank for its assistance in reaching this historic agreement. Informally, as key financiers of the World Bank, both the US and the UK had kept a close watch on the trilateral talks on the issue. The treaty was further strengthened by the setting up of a joint Indo–Pakistani Permanent Indus Commission in 1978 for regulating the distribution of waters with powers of arbitration.

SOVIET MEDIATION AND THE TASHKENT DECLARATION (1965–6)

The Soviet Union mediated between India and Pakistan against the backdrop of the short war between the two countries in September 1965. The war was caused by what India alleged as infiltration of about 3,000–4,000 Pakistanis in the Indian part of Kashmir to carry out guerrilla action and in violation of the CFL agreement of 1949. Pakistan claimed that it had not sent any infiltrators across the border. It attributed all arson, killings and sabotage to the uprising of the local Kashmiri population against repressive policies, especially the measures taken by the Indian government to fully integrate the state of Jammu & Kashmir into the Indian union. These measures involved application of Articles 356 and 357 of the Indian Constitution to Kashmir state, which enabled the president of India to establish President's Rule in Kashmir and legislate on some state subjects. The designation of the prime minister of Jammu & Kashmir was also abolished and replaced by that of chief minister, as in other Indian states. The legislative assembly of Jammu & Kashmir also adopted the constitutional amendments bill. Pakistan claimed that, as an aggrieved party in the Kashmir dispute, it had only moral links, if any, with this revolt. It persisted with this argument of its innocence before the Security Council, even though the UNMOGIP and independent observers documented the evidence of massive infiltration of armed personnel.

Islamabad's military strike in the Chamb and the Poonch areas in August 1965, ostensibly aimed at securing Kashmir through military means, triggered Indian response and the beginning of the 22-days' war on 1 September 1965. India seized the passes and territory on the Pakistani side of the CFL from where the infiltrators were entering Kashmir. Pakistan reacted by sending armoured columns across the LOC in southern Kashmir. India extended the conflict by crossing the recognized international boundary in Punjab. The fighting between the Indian and Pakistani troops continued for the next three weeks along the West Pakistan–India border. The 1965 war was not decisive as it did not conclude in clear victory for any one side. However, when the UN arranged a ceasefire, India seemed to be in an advantageous position because a large quantity of the US-supplied Pakistani armour was destroyed in the war. This made the Indian armed forces feel more secure, and restored their morale shaken after the defeat in the war with China in 1962. The Indians also held a commanding position near the Pakistani city of Lahore, causing a serious threat to Pakistani security.

Soviet Prime Minister Alexei Kosygin offered his good offices to India and Pakistan even as the war was on in early September 1965. After the end of the war, the Soviets renewed the offer and attempted to broker a peace agreement. What Kosygin offered was not active mediation, but assistance in bilateral dialogue at a location in the USSR acceptable to both India and Pakistan. The USSR had been a reluctant and infrequent mediator in international conflicts. It had enough reasons to make such an offer, as continuation of the India–Pakistan conflict threatened its own strategic interests in the region. It was a high-stakes and low-risk opportunity for the communist power, its first major mediation effort since World War II. After the growing Chinese proximity to Pakistan and the emergence of the Soviet–Chinese divide, the USSR needed an opportunity to neutralize the Chinese advance in South Asia. Besides, its success in mediation would not only help increase its leverage *vis-à-vis* India and Pakistan, but also contain American power in the region. After the end of the Khrushchev regime, the new government in Moscow was keen to strengthen its relationship with India, while at the same time remove misgivings on the Pakistani side. Kosygin had developed a good rapport with Ayub Khan during the latter's visit to Moscow in April 1965. This personal rapport was by far responsible for the acceptance of the USSR as a mediator. The US, on its part, had no objection to the USSR performing a mediatory role as it was itself not ready for such a task, being preoccupied with the developments in the Middle East and the ongoing Vietnam war. Moreover, both India and Pakistan were bitter with the US for cutting off aid and military supplies during the war which had affected their war preparedness.[5]

The summit conference between Indian Prime Minister Lal Bahadur Shastri and Pakistani President Ayub Khan took place at Tashkent from 4 to 10 January 1966. The Soviet mediation was more procedural than substantive. Kosygin had consciously refrained from conveying his own views on the likely solution of the Kashmir dispute. He even kept away from the discussions between the two leaders and their delegations for the first two days, but when the summit seemed headed for a failure, he took control of the conference and held separate talks with Shastri and Ayub Khan in order to make them agree to a draft agreement. Soviet Foreign Minister Andrei Gromyko also held intensive dialogue with India's Minister for External Affairs Swaran Singh and with Pakistan's Foreign Minister Zulfikar Ali Bhutto. Kosygin's persuasive powers finally succeeded in breaking the deadlock. The Tashkent Declaration was signed on 10 January 1966. The declaration bound both the countries: to settle their disputes peacefully and in accordance with the principles of the UN Charter; respect the CFL and return their troops to the positions they held prior to 5 August 1965; to not interfere in each other's internal affairs; restore trade and economic relations; and make

[5] Thomas Perry Thornton, 'The Indo-Pakistani Conflict: Soviet Mediation at Tashkent 1966', in Saadia Touval and I. William Zartman (eds.), *International Mediation in Theory and Practice*, Boulder: Westview Press, 1985, p. 144.

arrangements for the repatriation of prisoners of war. The agreement became possible due to the desire of all three parties to make it possible. India, Pakistan and the USSR had stakes in the success of the conference. If the Indian and the Pakistani leaders returned empty-handed without any commitment from the other side they would have been considered weak. Failure of the summit would have also impaired the credibility of the Soviet Union and its leverage with India and Pakistan.

The Tashkent Declaration carried a lot of symbolic importance. It was the first major agreement between the two states which committed them to a peaceful resolution of their conflict. The declaration generated a mood of optimism among international observers, though the public reaction in India and Pakistan was not complimentary. The opinion makers in both the states felt that an opportunity to extract substantial concessions from the other side was lost. Accusations and counter-accusations began to be traded within weeks of the signing of the declaration. Not surprisingly, India and Pakistan referred to the spirit of the Tashkent Declaration only rarely, and did not consider the commitments made therein worth taking seriously. Obviously, the future relationship between them was not to be guided by the promise made by Shastri and Ayub at the Tashkent Municipal Hall on the evening of 10 January 1966 to refrain from hostile propaganda against each other and work for peace in accordance with the principles of the UN.

ARBITRATION IN THE DISPUTE OVER THE RANN OF KUTCH (1965–8)

India and Pakistan have used international arbitration to settle their conflicting claims over the Rann of Kutch, a vast marshy land of some 8,400 square miles in the state of Gujarat in western India along the India–Pakistan border. Originally an extension of the Arabian Sea, the area was closed off and converted into a salty marsh by centuries of silting. As the Rann was the bone of contention between the princely state of Kutch and the British Indian province of Sindh, the Radcliffe Commission on the demarcation of the boundary between the two states at the time of Partition did not give a clear ruling on the Rann of Kutch. The historical records on the subject were also unclear. Pakistan put a claim on 3,500 square miles of this territory, arguing that the Rann was a lake rather than a marsh, hence the international norms of demarcation of boundary for lakes should apply to it. This claim was rejected by India as it believed that there was a well-established boundary running roughly along the northern edge of the Rann as shown in the pre-Partition maps.

The dispute led to military engagement between the two countries in 1956 in the Chhad Bet area of the Rann. The bilateral negotiations between the two governments on the issue in 1960 failed to result in any agreement. However, the two sides decided to collect and present further historical and cartographic data on their respective claims. There was a major engagement between the Indian and Pakistani armed forces in the area in April 1965. Following the offer of good offices by British Prime Minister Harold Wilson at the Commonwealth Prime Ministers' meeting, India and Pakistan agreed to a ceasefire, and concluded an agreement in June 1965 which stipulated that if there was no resolution of the dispute within two months, it would be submitted for arbitration by an international tribunal. As no agreement could be reached within the stipulated two months, India Pakistan Western Boundary Tribunal, consisting of one judge appointed by India (Alec Bebler of Yugoslavia), one judge appointed by Pakistan (Nasrollah Entezam of Iran), and the third judge jointly selected by these two judges (Gunnar Lagergren of Sweden), was constituted by the Secretary General of the UN. In its award made by a majority of two in February 1968, the tribunal awarded 350 square miles of the Rann area to Pakistan. Bebler submitted a dissenting note. Indian Prime Minister Indira Gandhi publicly expressed her dissatisfaction with the award, but decided to accept it in the spirit of arbitration. The new boundary between India and Pakistan (though not significantly different from the earlier one) in the Rann area was later demarcated by joint survey teams of India and Pakistan. However, the tribunal's award did not include

Sir Creek, a 60-km-long estuary in the Rann of Kutch. Both India and Pakistan are staking their claim this area based on their differing interpretations of the maritime boundary line dividing the creek.

ROLE OF THE US IN CONFLICT MANAGEMENT, CONFIDENCE BUILDING AND PREVENTIVE DIPLOMACY

Among the major powers of the world, the US has been involved most actively in the various regional conflicts in the post-World War II period. The logic of the Cold War required that such involvement and mediation become key elements of America's global strategy. Its superior power resources and worldwide strategic interests underpin its desire to mediate. More than any other power, it has mediated in conflicts in Asia, Latin and South America, the Middle East, Africa and Europe directly, or has been a major participant in UN mediation efforts.

It is, therefore, not surprising that the US has taken several initiatives over the last few decades to encourage India and Pakistan to resolve their disputes and manage their relations in a peaceful manner. Though South Asia was a traditionally low-priority area with the US, and South Asian geopolitics and problems remained somewhat remote from American public consciousness, the US had been involved with the affairs of India and Pakistan even before their Independence. President Franklin D. Roosevelt's steadfast espousal of the cause of Indian independence is well known. Having been involved with the affairs of India and Pakistan intimately from the beginning of their journeys and with the ups and down of their relationships, and enjoying considerable leverage over both, the US is probably in a more advantageous position to influence the two states than the other powers in the present scenario.

The change in the South Asian strategic environment after the Soviet invasion of Afghanistan in 1979 forced the US to arm Pakistan as a frontline state to confront the Soviets. As the USSR had signed a security and economic pact with India, the Soviet invasion of Afghanistan increased the threat perception of Pakistan *vis-à-vis* this alliance. The consequent infusion of massive American military and economic assistance including F-16 aircraft to Pakistan, in turn, raised the threat perceptions of India, which considered acquisition of these aircraft by Pakistan as directed against India rather than the Soviets. India began augmenting its own military equipments and arsenals by purchases from the Soviet Union, France, and other states. Washington was worried by the tensions developing in India–Pakistan relations due to the incipient arms race, threatening rhetorical stance of the leaders of the two states, and India's accusations of Pakistan's abetment of militancy in Punjab. The need for stability between India and Pakistan on the military front and prevention of war became acute and pressing as the US could ill afford a military conflict in a region where stability was essential for containing the Soviets. Interestingly, even as it provided unprecedented assistance to Pakistan, Washington was keen not to alienate India considering its size, importance in South Asia, and economic potential. If India and Pakistan were to go to war, America would have been forced to take any one country's side—a prospect it wanted to avoid at all costs.

With the end of the Cold War and the disintegration of the Soviet Union, the US emerged as the unchallenged leader of a coalition of Western powers dominating economic, security, and political affairs. The US foreign policy in the post-Cold War era has aimed at stabilizing conflict-prone regions and putting into effect a universal nuclear non-proliferation regime. Free from the compulsion of containing the Soviet influence in South Asia, the US began looking afresh at the evolving security scenario in the region and its political and economic relations with India and Pakistan. In view of the reports of the two states being 'a turn of the screwdriver away' from the making of an atomic bomb, containing India–Pakistan conflict and nuclear proliferation in the region became top priorities of America's South Asia policy. Military conflicts and nuclearization of South Asia directly threatened American interests and the stability of the unipolar world order it was attempting to maintain and strengthen.

The last one and a half decades have, therefore, witnessed persistent and high-profile American involvement in India–Pakistan relations. From the beginning of the 1990s, the US government periodically dispatched several senior government functionaries to advocate regional détente and resolution of bilateral disputes. America has exerted pressure on the two countries to come to the negotiating table and explore a settlement of the Kashmir problem. The summit meetings at Agra in 2001 and Islamabad in 2004 were believed to be the outcomes of American persuasion. The US has also been a principal outside actor in the preventive diplomacy carried out to defuse the serious crises between the two adversaries in the last few years. Preventive diplomacy is an effort to avoid the occurrence of conflicts between countries, to prevent existing conflicts from escalating into armed conflicts, and to prevent armed conflicts from expanding further.

The desire to halt formal nuclearization of South Asia and avoid the outbreak of military hostilities through miscalculation, misperception, accident or lack of communication was the key reason for America's persistent and forceful pursuit of an India–Pakistan Confidence Building Measures (CBM) regime on the lines of the East-West strategic relations. Such pursuit also resulted in some CBM agreements between India and Pakistan. American assistance to confidence building between India and China preceded the introduction of formal CBMs between India and Pakistan. Sino–Indian engagement with a CBM process began after the stand-off following a border skirmish between their armies in the Sumdorong Chu sector in late 1986. India also conducted a military exercise along the Sino–Indian border code-named Operation Checkerboard. This prompted Washington and Moscow to impress upon India and China to embark upon CBMs. The two countries agreed to maintain status quo along the Line of Actual Control (LAC) and set up a series of transparency measures, mainly relating to pre-notification of military exercises and information exchanges.

Operation Brasstacks

Operation Brasstacks, a mammoth exercise by the Indian Army undertaken in 1986–7, created a military crisis of dangerous proportions between India and Pakistan. Gen. Krishnaswami Sundarji, Chief of Staff of the Indian Army then, carried out a programme of modernization, structural rationalization, and improved mechanization of the land forces. Operation Brasstacks was designed with a vision to test the operational efficiency of the forces and equipments in this context.[6] It was also meant to test the coordination between the army, navy and air force. The military exercise included an India–Pakistan war game code-named Trident in which India made massive deployment of forces on the Rajasthan border. Pakistan misinterpreted the large concentration and exercise of the Indian troops and testing of weapons as India's preparation for war and retaliated by mobilizing its own troops, bringing them to forward positions and conducting a similar exercise along its border with India in Punjab. Indian High Commissioner to Pakistan S.K. Singh was summoned by Pakistan's Minister of State for Foreign Affairs Zain Noorani, on behalf of President Zia-ul Haq and told that Pakistan was 'capable of inflicting unacceptable damage' to India if the latter tried to violate its territorial integrity or sovereignty.[7] As Pakistan refused to withdraw its troops from forward positions even after the exercise was over, India also put its forces on high operational alert from 23 January 1987 onwards. This situation was fraught with the risk of escalation into an open military conflict. The crisis finally blew over with the intervention of the prime ministers of the two States, and subsequent discussions held between the foreign ministers and other high-ranking diplomats and military officials. The main cause of this avoidable military crisis was lack of prior communication between the Indian and Pakistani armed forces, and lack of co-

[6] Kanti Bajpai, P.R. Chari, Pervaiz Iqbal Cheema, Stephen Cohen and Sumit Ganguly, *Brasstacks and Beyond: Perception and Management of Crisis in South Asia*, New Delhi: Manohar, 1995.

[7] Jayantanuja Bandyopadhyaya, *The Making of India's Foreign Policy*, 3rd edn., New Delhi: Allied Publishers, 2003, p. 272.

ordination between India's Ministries of External Affairs and Defence.

After the Brasstacks crisis, America became more conscious of the need to develop an appropriate and balanced policy response to India–Pakistan relations. It even acted as an occasional intermediary between the two countries, sharing intelligence inputs with the two governments and exchanging information on the movement of the militaries of the two states.[8] Following the visit of US Defence Secretary Casper Weinberger, America sent a paper to the Indian and Pakistani governments in October 1986 detailing the European experience on CBMs, and urging the two states to implement such measures that were applicable and suitable to the South Asian situation.

The 1990 Military Crisis and CBMs

The renewal of militancy in Kashmir in 1989 also spurred American interest in CBMs in South Asia. The fear that the low-intensity conflict in Kashmir carried risk of escalation into a full-scale war came close to reality when, in February–March 1990, another military crisis and warlike situation was created by the Indian Army's mobilization for training and manoeuvres in the Mahajan range in Rajasthan, and the reported threat by Pakistan to use nuclear weapons to defeat an Indian attack. Though a steep escalation in the situation was prevented, the crisis added to the prevalent tension in Kashmir. An investigative story by Seymour Hersh in *The New Yorker* in March 1993 revealed that Pakistan evacuated fissionable material from the nuclear plant at Kahuta, and allegedly moved nuclear weapons in a truck convoy from their suspected storage facility in Baluchistan to an airbase during this crisis. However, serious observers dispute that the threat of a nuclear confrontation was very high, or that Pakistan had actually deployed nuclear weapons during the 1990 crisis.[9]

[8] Ibid., p. 82.

[9] Michael Krepon and Faruqee Mishi (eds.), *Conflict Prevention and Confidence Building Measures in South Asia: The 1990 Crisis*, Washington: The Henry L. Stimson Center, 1994, for details of a discussion held at the Stimson Center on the nuclear implications of the 1990 military crisis.

The US ambassadors to India and Pakistan played a conciliatory role during the 1990 crisis.[10] Recognizing the risks involved in leaving the dangers posed by the India–Pakistan conflict unaddressed, the US dispatched Deputy National Security Advisor Robert Gates to the two States in 1990, mainly to impress upon them to halt further development of their nuclear programmes and to establish nuclear risk reduction measures to obviate the chances of a nuclear incident due to accident or miscalculation. The Gates mission was helpful in mollifying India and Pakistan. During his visit in November 1990, US Under Secretary of State for International Security Affairs Reginald Bartholomew also suggested and discussed specific models of CBMs between India and Pakistan. These measures aimed at achieving nuclear nonproliferation, reduction of the defence budget and strength of the armed forces, accountability, and transparency.[11]

The changed realities of the post-Cold War era and the inevitable American leadership of the 'New World Order' enunciated by President George W. Bush had qualitatively altered perceptions about the US role in South Asia. India and Pakistan also reacted favourably to Washington's role as a facilitator for confidence building due to a genuine realization of the utility of these measures, as well as due to the apprehension that rejection of America's proposals entailed the risk of losing its goodwill. In the latter part of the tenure of President Bush, Special Assistant to the President and Senior Director of the Near East and South Asia Division of the National Security Council, Richard N. Hass also acted as an intermediary between India and Pakistan, urging then to settle the Kashmir dispute peacefully and further expand the CBMs.[12]

The two states agreed to provide advance notification of certain levels of military exercises to avoid accidental war, or a conflict resulting out of misinformation and misperception. After the 1990 military crisis, such an agreement was suggested by Pakistan

[10] Ibid.

[11] J.N. Dixit, *India-Pakistan in War and Peace*, New Delhi: Books Today, 2002, p. 159.

[12] Manoj Joshi, *The Lost Rebellion*, p. 317.

to avoid recurrence of a similar situation. It took nearly one year for India and Pakistan to conclude an agreement on this issue, Signed in 1991, the agreement clearly specifies the areas covered, the type of military exercises to be notified and the period before which this notice has to be sent. It also provides details about the notification of troops' movement on internal duties. Following the military crisis of 1990, it was decided to use the hotline, which was only sparingly used, on a weekly basis to enable the military functionaries of the two states to talk more frequently and exchange ideas relating to the mutual problems of the two militaries in various sectors along the India–Pakistan border. The air wings of the two militaries also set up a separate hotline in 1993. The two states also reached an agreement in April 1991 to not violate each other's airspace, to give advance notification of air exercises, and to follow agreed procedures for military flights near the border.

The US Role in the Kashmir Dispute

In the early 1960s, under the administration of President John F. Kennedy, the US tried to mediate between India and Pakistan for the settlement of the Kashmir problem outside the ongoing UN mediatory process. American Ambassador to India and Harvard economist John K. Galbraith played a stellar role in this effort.[13] Galbraith had several meetings with Prime Minister Nehru in this regard. It is believed that Kennedy had proposed the name of Eugene R. Black, former president of the World Bank, as a mediator.[14] Black had succeeded in bringing the two countries to settle their dispute over the Indus basin water issue. However, the US proposal on mediation was turned down by the Indian leadership. The global political scenario in the subsequent years, especially India's strong political and strategic ties with the Soviet Union, pushed India further down in the foreign policy priority of the American administrations. India also became critical of the American military and economic assistance to Pakistan in the 1970s

[13] Ibid., pp. 301–11.
[14] Ibid.

and the 1980s, as well as its pro-Pakistan stance. A serious role for America in the management and resolution of the Kashmir problem was thus ruled out.

America's activism on Kashmir was revived after the end of the Cold War. The first term of President Bill Clinton turned out to be particularly stormy for US efforts in India–Pakistan conflict resolution due to the statements and actions of US Assistant Secretary of State for South Asia Robin Raphel. It was reported in the *Indian Express* in December 1994 that the Dixon plan for the settlement of Kashmir proposed by the UN in 1951 was being revived by Raphel.[15] However, no one in the US, India or Pakistan officially confirmed or denied this. When asked about the US position on Kashmir, Raphel stated in a press meeting:

> Our view on the status of Kashmir has not changed. We still are of the view that the geographical area of former princely state of Jammu & Kashmir and the entire geographic area is disputed territory. Our view remains the same. In terms of the US role, we are of the view that the dispute over Kashmir needs to be resolved by India and Pakistan sitting at the table and seriously engaging in negotiations on that issue. We also believe that for any resolution to be stable and long-lasting, the wishes of the Kashmiri people have to be taken into account. Exactly how you do that it is not our place to prescribe.[16]

On the issue of American mediation in Kashmir, she replied:

> If both India and Pakistan wished for a more explicit US role in solving the Kashmir dispute we will be happy to do that. In Pakistan, we have often heard, for example, why don't you mediate as you have done in West Asia. I have always replied to that in order to be a mediator, you have to be accepted as such by both sides. In this case, we do not have that. Pakistan wishes it but India does not for its own reasons. Therefore, we have not been able to play a role. But we stand willing and, meanwhile, we do what we can to encourage the two governments to sit down and talk about it.[17]

[15] K.P. Nayar, 'U.S. Reviving Dixon Plan in Bid to End Kashmir Row', *Indian Express* (New Delhi), 19 December 1994.

[16] Quoted by Moonis Ahmar, *The Road to Peace in South Asia: Lessons for India and Pakistan from the Arab-Israeli Peace Process*, Urbana Champaign: University of Illinois, ACDIS Project, 1996, p. 41.

[17] Ibid.

Raphel's statements and her meetings with the leaders of some separatist organizations of Jammu & Kashmir aroused strong Indian reaction and gave a setback to America's efforts to nudge the two states towards reconciliation.

The question of the US acting as a mediator on Kashmir also led to intense lobbying among American Congressmen by the Indian and Pakistani governments. In September 1999, a group of America's Congressmen, including 16 Senators, wrote to President Bill Clinton to appoint a special envoy to mediate the conflict over Kashmir, which is 'the most dangerous nuclear flashpoint in the world today'.[18] This move was sponsored by Republican Congressman Dan Burton and Democrat Congressman David Bonior. Significantly, it also received support from Jesse Helms, the Republican Senator and chairperson of the Senate Foreign Relations Committee. India sought to counter Pakistan's lobbying in the American Congress. Hence, Republican Congressman Benjamin Gilman, chairman of the International Relations Committee in the House of Representatives, and the Democrat representative Sam Gejdenson published a letter urging Clinton to reject any call for third-party mediation by America, and cautioned him that such a move would severely impair regional security in South Asia rather than help resolve the conflict. Gary Ackerman, co-chairman of the Congressional Caucus on India and Indian Americans, also backed the Indian position on bilateralism in India–Pakistan negotiations.[19]

Part of the American leverage over India, lost due to the Robin Raphel episode and the imposition of sanctions following the nuclear tests at Pokhran in May 1998, was regained later due to Clinton's role in the Kargil conflict and his visit to South Asia in March 2000. Clinton's announcements during his visit made it amply clear that America would not like to impose itself as a mediator unless explicitly requested to do so by the two governments. However, it would continue its back-channel diplomacy to push India and Pakistan towards talking on Kashmir. In recent

[18] Keith Jones, 'India and Pakistan Vie for US's Favour': http://www.wsws.org/articles/1999/oct1999/ind-o01.shtml, 1 October 1999.

[19] Ibid.

months, the official American position has shifted perceptibly from Kashmir as a purely bilateral issue to solving Kashmir bilaterally with international assistance. To quote Richard Armitage: '(Kashmir) will be solved bilaterally, but I think with the help, and the assistance and encouragement of the international community, first among them the United States....'[20]

The Kargil Conflict

The Indian and Pakistani armies fought an intense battle in Kargil district along the LOC in Jammu & Kashmir in 1999. Conventionally, due to inhospitable weather and adverse conditions, the Indian Army used to vacate this mountainous region during winter, and return to defend it at the beginning of summer. Chances of infiltration by militants and breach of the LOC by the Pakistan Army were considered minimal in view of the unendurable weather conditions. However, much to its surprise, the Indian Army discovered in May 1999 that two brigades of the Pakistan Army comprising battalions of the Northern Light Infantry along with some irregular forces had crossed the LOC in the Kargil region (in the Dras, Batalik, Mushkoh, Kaksar, Turtok and Chorbat La sectors) in Kashmir, and had moved in to a depth of about 10 km. The infiltrators even lived in the bunkers meant for Indian soldiers. The *jihadi* infiltrators, belonging to Pakistan, Afghanistan, Libya, Sudan and some other Muslim countries, were given armed and logistical support by the Pakistan Army. Many of the intruders were Pakistan Army regulars. Initially, Pakistan argued that it had nothing to do with these infiltrators who were members of the *mujahideen* forces fighting for freedom in Kashmir. However, it was soon confirmed that this infiltration was part of the Pakistan Army's Operation Badr to cross the LOC during winter, when the Indian Army abandoned its bunkers and defensive posts. The probable motives of Pakistan in doing so were to get the Kashmir issue internationalized, and take retaliatory action against India's control of the Siachen Glacier region in 1984. India launched Operation Vijay to restore the LOC and vacate encroachments by

[20] Editorial, *Times of India* (New Delhi), 12 June 2002.

the Pakistan Army and the Kashmiri militants. The Indian military response triggered a full-scale armed operation between the two States in Jammu & Kashmir, a semi-war along the 200-km range of the LOC that lasted from May 1999 till the end of July 1999.

The Kargil conflict was brought to an end by US President Bill Clinton. After initial uncertainty, international opinion had turned against Pakistan for crossing the LOC. Indian Prime Minister Atal Behari Vajpayee sent his personal envoy and National Security Adviser Brajesh Misra with a letter to meet Clinton and apprise him of the Indian position on the issue, and his government's expectation that America would restrain Pakistan's adventurism in Kargil. Clinton seemed to concur with the Indian position on the need for maintaining the sanctity of the LOC. He dispatched Gen. Anthony Zinni, Commander-in-Chief of the US Central Command, and Deputy Assistant Secretary of State Gibson Lanpher to Islamabad in June 1999 to discuss the possibilities of defusing the tension with Pakistani civilian and military officers, and work out the mechanics of a ceasefire. He also categorically asked the Pakistan Prime Minister Nawaz Sharif during the latter's visit to Washington in early July 1999 to pull back his army from Kargil, and respect the LOC as per the provisions of the Simla accord. According to media reports, US National Security Advisor Sandy Berger held telephonic discussions with his Indian counterpart Brajesh Misra regarding the joint US–Pakistan statement to be issued at the end of Sharif's visit, while Clinton called Vajpayee during his meeting with Sharif.[21] The July 1999 meeting in Washington, has even been described as a 'miniaturized Camp David'.[22] The joint US–Pakistan statement also mentioned Clinton's 'personal interest in encouraging an expeditious resumption and intensification' of bilateral efforts to find a settlement of India–Pakistan disputes. For many, Clinton's 'personal interest' was a euphemism for the third-party role that the US played and wished

[21] Aijaz Ahmad, 'Mediation by any Other Name', *Frontline*: http://www.flonnet.com/fl1615/16150180.htm, 17–30 July 1999.

[22] Ibid.

to continue playing in this conflict. The US is also believed to have influenced the Chinese not to support Pakistan's actions in the Kargil war.[23]

The Terrorist Attack on the Indian Parliament and Threat of War

On 13 December 2001, there was a terrorist attack on the Indian Parliament by members of the Lashkar-e-Toiba and Jaish-e-Mohammed, two prominent Pakistan-based Kashmiri extremist outfits. These terrorists were prevented from causing a loss of life of the top rung of Indian leadership due to the swift action of the security forces. Horrified by this outrage and attack on the highest seat of power, the Government of India charged that its investigations pointed to irrefutable evidence of the strong links of these terrorists with the Pakistani intelligence agencies. The Indian government launched Operation Parakram, a massive mobilization of the armed forces of about 7,00,000 troops, along the borders with Pakistan in full war preparedness. The forces were kept ready to launch a strike at the shortest notice. Pakistan's counter-mobilization of its forces on the border resulted in the two armies at 'eyeball-to-eyeball' distance. Though war was not spelt out clearly as an option, there was an unmistakable indication that direct military action could be launched to destroy the 'infrastructure of terrorism' in Pakistan if it did not stop training, aiding and abetting terrorist groups. India also forwarded a list of the 20 most wanted persons who were accused of involvement in major acts of terrorism in India, and who were believed to be hiding in Pakistan, with a demand that they be handed over to India forthwith. To put further diplomatic pressure on Pakistan, India recalled its high commissioner to Pakistan.

Sensing that this snowballing tension could lead to war at a time when stability in the region was needed to carry out its fight against Osama bin Laden and global terrorism, and when Pakistan had rendered critical assistance in America's war against the Taliban regime in Afghanistan, the US played a major role in

[23] Dixit, *India–Pakistan in War and Peace*, p. 69.

crisis de-escalation. The Indian government made it clear that unless the US pressurized Pakistan to permanently end its support to terrorism against India, the security situation in South Asia could deteriorate beyond America's power to control. The US, on its part, put the Lashkar-e-Toiba and the Jaish-e-Mohammed on the list of terrorist organizations prepared by the Department of State and froze their assets in the US. It also tried to convince Pakistan's President Pervez Musharraf of the need to contain the Islamic fundamentalist groups operating from Pakistan.

Following America's counsel, Musharraf made a televised speech on 12 January 2002 reaffirming the commitment of his government to end terrorism and rein in the fundamentalist groups. However, he refused to give up Pakistan's long-standing political and moral support for the people fighting for the cause of Kashmir's freedom. The Musharraf regime also arrested key leaders of some terrorist groups. Consequently, India decided to give the Pakistani president some time to 'convert his words into action', and postpone direct military action against Pakistan. To consolidate the gains of a letdown in the tense situation, US Secretary of State Colin Powell and Defence Secretary Donald Rumsfeld visited India and Pakistan to further the normalization process. However, this mediatory effort could not be very fruitful, as the terrorist incidents against India's civilian population and the armed forces did not stop despite Musharraf's brave words against the so-called *jihadi* forces.

Attack on the Army Camp at Kaluchak

On 14 May 2002 the terrorists struck at the Indian Army camp at Kaluchak near Jammu, resulting in the killing of a number of Indian Army soldiers and their family members. The attack coincided with the visit of US Assistant Secretary of State for South Asia Christina Rocca to the subcontinent. The Indian government charged that all those involved in this attack came from Pakistan and had received their training on Pakistani soil. Alerted by the incensed opinion of the Indian public and political parties, the Vajpayee government gave an ultimatum to Pakistan to stop abetting terrorism, failing which war would be unavoidable.

The US and the UK played a role in facilitating crisis management after this terrorist attack. They also offered to have joint patrolling and monitoring of the LOC in Jammu & Kashmir with the Indian military forces. The visit of US Deputy Secretary of State Richard Armitage and Defence Secretary Donald Rumsfeld to New Delhi and Islamabad in early June 2002 was helpful in averting war. British Foreign Secretary Jack Straw, the European Union's Commissioner on External Affairs Chris Patten, Iranian Foreign Minister Kamal Kharrazi, and Japanese Senior Foreign Minister Seiken Suguira also visited the subcontinent to defuse the crisis, and advised restraint to India and Pakistan. Russian President Vladimir Putin offered to help settle the differences between the two states, and suggested that Indian Prime Minister Vajpayee and Pakistan President Musharraf meet each other at the Conference on Interaction and Confidence Building Measures at Almaty, Kazakhstan, in June 2002. While Pakistan welcomed the Russian offer of mediation, India ruled out any possibility of Tashkent II.

The Agra Summit

Indian Prime Minister Atal Behari Vajpayee invited Pakistan's military ruler Pervez Musharraf in May 2001 for a summit meeting. Following the acceptance of this invitation, the two leaders met at the historic city of Agra from 14–16 July 2001. The US played a crucial behind-the-scenes role in organizing this summit. Surprisingly, even the dates of the summit were announced first by the US Department of State rather than by the Indian or Pakistan governments. Musharraf declared before coming to India that the summit was being organized due to American pressure. India strongly denied this statement. However, the diplomatic activity prior to the summit gave a different picture. After playing an active role in bringing the hostilities to an end in Kargil, the US was keen that India and Pakistan resume their dialogue on all bilateral issues. The US was sending signals to the Indian and Pakistani officials who separately visited Washington, in the months prior to the summit. Following the announcement of the summit, top Indian and Pakistani officials visited Washington and met their US counterparts. In mid-June, Pakistan Foreign Minister Abdul Sattar met US Secretary of State Colin Powell and his deputy Richard Armitage and assured them of Pakistan's desire to talk peace with India and crack down on terrorism. Later, Vajpayee's Principal Secretary and National Security Adviser Brajesh Misra met State Department officials as well as Vice-President Richard Cheney, National Security Advisor Condoleeza Rice, and CIA Director George Tenet. It was even believed that the US had prepared and submitted a proposed draft of the joint declaration to be issued at the end of the summit.[24]

The Agra Summit was probably the most planned summit in the history of India–Pakistan relations. In order to gain legitimacy at the summit, Gen. Musharraf crowned himself the President of Pakistan removing the civilian President Rafiq Tarar on 20 June 2001. Prior to the summit, India also announced many unilateral goodwill measures like the relaxation of visa norms for Pakistani citizens, release of Pakistani fishermen arrested for entering Indian maritime areas, and removal of curbs on items imported from Pakistan. The summit aroused high hopes and media attention about India–Pakistan rapprochement. The media created such hype around the summit as if some historic U-turn in India–Pakistan relations was going to take place—a sort of breaking of the Berlin Wall in South Asia.

However, the summit ended in failure. This did not cause surprise as the meeting was held without any specified agenda for negotiations. Indeed, agenda-setting in India–Pakistan relations itself has been a contentious issue. Discussing what to discuss led to polarized standpoints at Agra. India insisted on a comprehensive set of issues, including cross-border terrorism, opening up of trade, cultural exchanges, and removal of visa restrictions. Musharraf, on the other hand, was keen on discussing only one issue, i.e. the 'core issue' of Kashmir. In his press conference, brushing

[24] M.R. Mulkani, 'Agra's Bitter Aftertaste', *Hindustan Times*, 18 August 2001.

aside Indian concerns on terrorism, he even described this terrorism as a 'freedom struggle'. The differences in the approaches of the two sides were so grave that, let alone any agreement, even the ritualistic joint declaration at its end could not be issued, and Musharraf left India a day earlier than scheduled.

The failure of the Agra Summit proved that atmospherics—smiles, embraces, body language and hospitality—work only up to a point between states. A summit should be regarded as a culmination of slow and sustained diplomacy, rather than as its beginning. It is advisable to check unfettered expectations, media exposure and optimism prior to any future India–Pakistan dialogue. Such bilateral meetings should be approached with cautious optimism, tinged with realistic recognition of the thorny complexities of the India–Pakistan conflict.

The Islamabad Summit

Leaving behind the failure of the Agra Summit and the sharp deterioration in relations following the attack on the Indian Parliament in December 2001, India and Pakistan used the opportunity of the SAARC Summit at Islamabad in January 2004 to resume top-level contacts and further the process of confidence building. Greater caution and better preparation than what was seen at the Agra Summit marked the peace initiative this time. India and Pakistan announced a ceasefire across the border in Kashmir in November 2003. On the eve of the summit, India offered a package of CBMs designed to widen people-to-people contacts. The proposed CBMs included transport links between Srinagar on the Indian side of Kashmir and Muzaffarabad on the Pakistan side, as well as between Munabao in the state of Rajasthan and Khokrapar in Sindh. Formerly a major trade route for the Himalayan region, the Muzaffarabad–Srinagar highway was closed in 1948 following the first war between Pakistan and India. The other major proposal made by New Delhi related to increase in the strength of the high commission staff in Islamabad and New Delhi, and lifting of restrictions imposed on the movement of the Pakistan High Commission employees in the aftermath of the terrorist attack on Parliament.

Compared to Agra, President Musharraf's position had been strengthened by the American support to his regime and the legitimacy he had gained through a popular referendum and vote of confidence from Pakistan's Parliament. Spontaneity and sincerity marked the joint statement issued after the summit, at which India and Pakistan agreed to resume their composite dialogue on all bilateral issues, including Jammu & Kashmir, from February 2004. The 'Kashmir-first approach' was not emphasized much by Pakistan, which showed greater sensitivity to the composite dialogue process. Besides, while noting that the people of Kashmir must be involved in finding a solution to their problems in some form at some stage in the peace process, the president of Pakistan reassured that he would not permit any territory under Pakistan's control to be used for terrorism in any manner. Pakistan also adopted the Protocol on Terrorism along with other SAARC states at the Islamabad meeting. The protocol voices concerns about the debilitating threat of terrorism, in all its forms and manifestations, to the South Asian region, and reaffirms the commitment of the member countries to implement the SAARC convention on suppression of terrorism as well as other international conventions to which the members are parties. However, all these goodwill measures decided at Islamabad were more in the nature of a declaration of intent rather than a detailed indication of the pathway to peace in South Asia. To become meaningful, the peace process initiated in January 2004 needs many more steps and sustenance of the dialogue process that began after the summit.

The external powers, especially the US and the UK, played a facilitating role in the months preceding the summit. Without naming the US, Pakistan Prime Minister Jamali said that the current peace process had been facilitated by other countries. The US government offered a $3 billion aid package to Musharraf in June 2003, making it conditional upon 'cooperation in the war on terrorism', improved relations with India, and introduction of measures to promote internal democratization. US Secretary of State Colin Powell also wrote around the time of the summit that the US did not want to become a mediator in the India–Pakistan dispute, but would prefer to capitalize on the trust it had built with New Delhi and Islamabad to nudge both sides towards conciliation in a peaceful manner.[25]

OUTSIDE INITIATIVES FOR THE TRACK II PROCESS

The process of confidence building between India and Pakistan during the 1990s was facilitated a great deal by formal and informal Track II contacts at the non-governmental levels involving strategic thinkers, scholars, retired military officers and former diplomats of the two states. Former US diplomat Joseph Montville, who coined the term Track II in 1981, has given an extensive definition of Track II diplomacy.

> Track two diplomacy is unofficial, informal interaction between members of adversary groups of nations which aim to develop strategies, influence public opinion, and organize human and material resources in ways that might help resolve their conflicts. It must be understood that track two diplomacy is in no way a substitute for official, formal, 'track one' government-to-government or leader-to-leader relationship. Rather, track two activity is designed to assist official leaders by compensating for the constraints imposed on them by the psychologically understandable need for leaders to be, or at least to be seen to be, strong, wary and indomitable in the face of the enemy.[26]

Ideally, Track I process or official diplomacy should be able to solve disputes between nations. However, in an intractable conflict situation, official diplomacy might prove insufficient—or even deficient—in altering the perceptions of the participants in a conflict which is required for successful conflict management and

[25] Colin Powell, 'US Strategy for Partnerships', *Foreign Affairs*: http://www.foreignaffairs.org/20040101faessay83104/colin-l-powell/a-strategy-of-partnerships.html, January–February 2004.

[26] Joseph Montville, 'The Arrow and the Olive Branch: The Case for Track Two Diplomacy', in J. McDonald and D. Bendahmane (eds.), *Conflict Resolution: Track Two Diplomacy*, Washington: Foreign Service Institute, US Department of State, 1987, p. 7.

resolution. Such alteration could occur only when contacts take place informally. Track II diplomacy is aimed at bringing about such perceptual changes. It is carried out in an unofficial and flexible setting. Since it is unofficial, it is more likely to be accepted by people of different orientations.

While Track I and Track II processes run parallel, they are not expected to operate in isolation from or contrary to each other. Track II *supplements* the negotiations that are carried out between government officials and political leaders. Since the discussions in Track II meetings are held in an informal and cooperative setting, they are less constrained by the rigidity, limitations and compulsions underpinning official dialogues. The role of participants in such meetings is to define the problem, be innovative about possible solutions, and exert pressure on the governments through formal or informal means. The deliberations of Track II meetings should be kept away from the glare of publicity and media attention to give a certain latitude to the participants to be honest and frank in their ideas.

One of the earliest examples of Track II diplomacy at the international level was the Pugwash Conferences between the former officials of the US and the USSR who met at Pugwash, Canada, in the early 1950s to discuss contentious issues between their countries. Later, such meetings became larger, with the participation of scientists, military officers and professionals. Another attempt at unofficial diplomacy between the US and the USSR was the Dartmouth Conferences at Dartmouth, New Hampshire, from 1960 onwards.[27]

Alarmed by the downward drift in India–Pakistan relations, the US facilitated a Track II dialogue process in the 1990s between India and Pakistan to supplement its efforts for reconciliation directed at the two governments. The US had organized similar dialogues in the Middle East between Arab and Israeli participants. As the first step, the US Information Service (USIS) organized an

[27] John Burton and Frank Dukes, *Conflict: Practices in Management, Settlement and Resolution*, Houndmills and London: Macmillan, 1990, p. 140.

informal discussion between the retired military officials and diplomats of India and Pakistan at Neemrana, a historical fort in Rajasthan bordering Delhi, in 1991. Subsequent meetings in this series were held at other places in India and Pakistan. These meetings, symbolizing the initiation of non-governmental involvement in the India–Pakistan peace process, came to be known as the Neemrana Dialogues.

The 12 rounds of Neemrana Dialogues were moderated by a former American diplomat, Paul Kreisberg, and co-chaired by A.M. Khusro, a former member of the Planning Commission of India. It was hoped that such discussions would prove beneficial in generating new ideas for managing and resolving the India–Pakistan conflict, and that the participants, who were influential persons having close contacts with their respective governments, would transmit the problem-solving ideas discussed at such meetings to the respective policy makers. The Neemrana process was later converted into a travelling seminar by the USIS to involve people outside Delhi and younger participants from different backgrounds.

The interface between Track I and Track II has not been very close in South Asia. The channelling of ideas and decisions of Track II diplomacy to the ministries of Foreign Affairs and Defence is improbable. Unlike the US and other Western countries, the organizational structures of the foreign policy establishments in India and Pakistan is such that there is no scope for outsiders—scholars, journalists, retired diplomats and others—to influence or participate in the official decision-making processes. It is, therefore, doubtful if the retired diplomats and military commanders who participated in the Track II meetings exercised influence on their former colleagues in the ministries and armed forces after their retirement. There were, of course, exceptions among the participants of the Neemrana Dialogues, like I.K. Gujral, who rose to become India's Prime Minister, and Niaz Naik, who exercised considerable sway over policy making in Pakistan in the subsequent period, including his actions as an emissary between Nawaz Sharif and Atal Behari Vajpayee during the Kargil conflict.

OFFERS OF MEDIATION FROM OTHER STATES

Apart from the US, several other countries have offered to help India and Pakistan find an amicable solution to their problems. These states have also played a role to prevent the conflict and distrust between India and Pakistan from growing into a full-scale war. The UK, Iran, South Africa, Nepal, Bangladesh, the United Arab Emirates and Saudi Arabia have offered at various points of time to mediate or extend 'good offices' and 'assistance' for peaceful resolution of disputes between India and Pakistan. However, India has turned down all these offers on the principle that it subscribes to a bilateral approach in its dealings with Pakistan.

CHAPTER 4

Positions of India and Pakistan on Third-party Intervention

INDIA'S POSITION ON INTERNATIONAL MEDIATION

Though in the beginning India allowed a role for third parties in the Kashmir dispute and in the management of its relations with Pakistan, it has resolutely and consistently opposed any suggestion of formal mediation in India–Pakistan conflicts since the India–Pakistan war of 1971. A commitment to settle the disputes between the two states through bilateral negotiations was extracted from Pakistan Prime Minister Zulfikar Ali Bhutto and incorporated in the Simla Agreement of 1972. The memorandum of understanding attached with the Lahore Declaration of 1999 also enjoined the two states to engage in bilateral consultations on security concerns, nuclear doctrines, and reduction in arms and non-proliferation issues. India believes that morally and legally, Pakistan cannot abandon the explicit commitment to bilateralism made in the Simla Agreement and the Lahore Declaration. It is also the reason why India never misses reference to these two accords in the context of its ties with Pakistan.

Several governments have been in power in New Delhi since then, but the Indian stand on dealing with Pakistan within the bilateral framework of the Simla Agreement and opposition to formal international mediation has remained constant. India's insistence on bilateralism is unlikely to be reviewed in the foreseeable future, as near unanimity prevails among major political parties on this issue. The government, the media, politicians, commentators and the masses in India have been so sensitive to the issue of third-party initiative that even inoffensive and well-meaning proposals of friendly states like Russia, South Africa, Nepal and Iran to provide assistance in settling India's problems with Pakistan have been interpreted as threatening to India's sovereignty, integrity and vital national interests. India has favoured a bilateral approach with respect to not only Pakistan, but also with other South Asian states. Bilateralism has become one of the core principles of India's regional policy. The end of the Cold War and change in the international strategic environment seem to have had little influence on India's insistence on bilateralism. Possibly, the end of the Soviet support on India's Kashmir policy at the UN and other international forums might have enhanced India's sense of vulnerability with regard to international involvement in Kashmir, and its ability to fight overt Western support to Pakistan.

REASONS FOR INDIA'S ADVOCACY OF BILATERALISM

BILATERAL APPROACH IS PREFERABLE TO MEDIATION

India has argued that as the conflict is between India and Pakistan, others cannot be expected to resolve it for them. Mediation would encourage needless dependence on outsiders. Such dependence is avoidable because, in spite of the hostility and enmity in their relations, normal diplomatic channels between India and Pakistan have rarely got so strained as to require the good offices of another power to provide communication with the other party. Important agreements like the Simla pact, the Lahore Declaration, and the agreements on several confidence building measures between the two states have been concluded without direct participation of a third party.

Besides, the bilateral approach seems to be in the best interest of India and the South Asian region because it is able to 'take into account the unique features of each relationship' with individual South Asian states, and avoid 'any situation where all the other countries could unite against her'.[1] The diplomatic strategy of bilateralism also helps avoid internationalization of contentious issues in South Asia and avoid involvement of multiple actors in the region.[2] Such a strategy facilitates Indian ascendancy over South

[1] Harish Kapur, *India's Foreign Policy 1947–1992: Shadows and Substance*, New Delhi: Sage, 1994, p. 101.

[2] Ibid.

Asia. Formal intervention of outside powers in the affairs of the region, in the garb of mediation or multilateral diplomacy, could be inimical to the strategic and economic stability of South Asia and seriously impair Indian influence in the region. As an Indian strategic studies expert argues:

> The bilateral approach remains the best for tackling bilateral differences and problems, even as embryonic efforts to evolve a regional framework for security issues have been made in some parts of the world. The bilateral approach provides the most direct method to articulate national interests, resolve disputes peacefully, deter potential aggression, create new trade and investment opportunities, and to broaden national influence.[3]

Mediation might have been successful in mitigating certain other international conflicts, especially in the Middle East. But the strategic experience of one region cannot be easily transplanted to another region, because the success of third-party mediation depends upon several contextual factors. India also apprehends that mediation by an external power could undermine its negotiating power and strengthen Pakistan's bargaining position. The contemporary changes in the global security environment have not affected the nature of the India–Pakistan conflict. The conclusion of the Cold War might have caused an alteration in the motives and interests of the potential mediators, but it has not transformed the motives and interests of India and Pakistan. There is, therefore, no special case to argue for the increased probability of third-party role in India–Pakistan conflict in the current era.

Self-interested Advocacy of Mediation

Mediation is not a moral means of conflict resolution, but an instrument of foreign policy for the furtherance of one's goals and interests in international politics. No mediation effort, therefore, can be free from the realist considerations of security and power. The suggestions emanating from Western states for medi-

[3] Brahma Chellaney, 'CBMs: A Critical Appraisal', in Dipankar Banerji (ed.), *Confidence Building Measures in South Asia*, Colombo: Regional Centre for Strategic Studies, 1999, p. 24.

ated settlement of India–Pakistan conflict are not borne out of genuine desire for peace and stability, but out of the threat this conflict poses to the unipolar world order dominated by the coalition of Western countries. India and Pakistan, therefore, need not invest too much energy and hopes in mediation when the Western states themselves have followed it selectively, and only when it satisfied their own strategic interests. America and its allies did not rely upon third-party intervention or the UN to defuse the crises arising out of Iraq's occupation of Kuwait, Yugoslav dictator Milosevic's policies in Kosovo, refusal of the Taliban regime of Afghanistan to hand over Osama bin Laden after attacks on the World Trade Center and the Pentagon, or the presumed weapons of mass destruction in possession of Iraqi dictator Saddam Hussein. In other words, states like India, Pakistan, Israel and Egypt are persuaded or pressurized by the major powers to avoid war through mediation, while they themselves would not accept the mediation of others, in order to guard their own national interests. The question that needs to be addressed is: What are the criteria for determining when and in what type of conflicts mediation is to be applied or war is to be allowed? When the major powers themselves have followed unilateral, bilateral or multilateral approaches to peace in regional conflicts, depending upon their specific national interests, India need not feel apologetic about rejecting mediation with Pakistan.

Kashmir is not Subject to Mediation

The Indian resistance to the proposal of international mediation on Kashmir also stems from the fear that the acceptance of such mediation constitutes an indirect admission that Kashmir is a disputed territory, and that there is something to mediate on Kashmir, a position that India has challenged all through on the ground that Jammu & Kashmir is an integral and constitutionally indissoluble part of India which has acceded to the Indian Union in the same fashion as the other Indian provinces have. Mediation could be the beginning of a spiral of similar demands for self-determination and secession from other discontented regions.

Neutrality of Mediators

A major problem with international mediation is the neutrality of the mediators. Ideally, the mediators should not have any economic or political interests of their own in the conflict or in its resolution. They should not have been associated with one of the parties more favourably than with the other. They must enjoy trust and credibility with both the disputants to be able to carry on the mediation process. However, mediators rarely conform to this ideal of neutrality in reality. India believes that having honest, impartial and neutral mediators is nearly impossible in international politics. Instead of remaining neutral, mediators act as equal participants in the conflict along with the two parties, and seek to advance or protect their national interests through mediatory interventions. Hence, mediation is seen by many in India as a conspiracy of the Western states to secure economic and strategic benefit in the region.

THE INDIAN VIEW ON UN MEDIATION IN INDIA–PAKISTAN CONFLICT

India's reference of the Kashmir dispute to the UN in 1948 first began the process of internationalization of the Kashmir issue and mediation by external actors in India–Pakistan conflict. However, the Indian leadership soon realized the mistake of approaching the UN, and became lukewarm in extending support to the UN mediators and interlocutors. In retrospect, few among the scholars, diplomats and policy makers of India justify this reference to the UN; indeed, most regard it as one of India's biggest foreign policy blunders. It is also believed that Jawaharlal Nehru's decision to refer the Kashmir dispute to the UN Security Council was influenced by the advice he received from the last British Viceroy in India, Lord Mountbatten.[4] Nehru had initially expressed reservations about taking the issue to the UN, but was prevailed upon by Mountbatten to do so.

[4] J.N. Dixit, *Anatomy of a Flawed Inheritance: Indo-Pak Relations 1970–1994*, New Delhi: Konark, 1995, pp. 212–13.

Even Mahatma Gandhi, the 'Father of the Indian Nation', had reservations about the involvement of a third party like the UN or an arbitrator in Kashmir. In his prayer meeting on 25 December 1947, the Mahatma questioned the usefulness of arbitration in Kashmir. He cautioned that instead of resulting in a settlement of the dispute, this would merely introduce a third party into it. 'Can we not settle the issue between ourselves?' he had said.[5] When the Indian government, after gaining an upper hand in the fight against the infiltrators in Kashmir, formally lodged a complaint with the UN Security Council in January 1948, Gandhi commented, 'Whether they are right in doing so or not, God alone knows.' He said instead of UN-sponsored mediation, the two dominions should come together with 'God as witness' and find a settlement. Terming foreign influence as disastrous, he said 'that will be the worst imaginable fate for us. I shudder to think of it.'[6]

The experience with UN mediation on Kashmir and the attitude of the Western powers, particularly the US and the UK, in the late 1940s and the 1950s have strengthened India's stand against a third-party role. In its view, the UN adopted a pro-Pakistani stand from the beginning, not so much on the basis of the merits of the case, but because of Pakistan's key role in the emerging strategic interests of the US-led military blocs in South and Central Asia, viz., the South-East Asian Treaty Organization (SEATO) and the Baghdad Pact (CENTO) during the early years of the Cold War. Nehru found the UN unsuitable for the task of mediation within weeks of India lodging the complaint against Pakistan. He stated on 15 February 1948 that 'instead of discussing and deciding on our reference in a straightforward manner, the nations of the world sitting in that body got lost in power politics'.[7] By the late 1950s, India had realized that it was futile to expect the controlling powers of the UN to understand the

[5] 'Mahatma was against Third Party Role': http://www.rediff.com/news/1998/jun/05mg.htm, 5 June 1998.

[6] Ibid.

[7] Prime Minister Jawaharlal Nehru's statement reported in *The Hindu* (Chennai [earlier Madras]), 16 February 1948 and cited by A. Appadorai and M.S. Rajan, *India's Foreign Policy and Relations*, New Delhi: South Asian Publishers, 1985, p. 92.

Indian position on Kashmir. Hence, for all practical purposes, India paid only formal and ritualistic attention to UN efforts at resolving the Kashmir issue.

The Security Council also seemed obsessed with the idea of implementing the resolutions on Jammu & Kashmir passed by it between 1948 and 1950 rather than addressing the changed material and political realities. This legalistic approach contradicted the flexibility expected of a mediation effort. Pakistan's refusal to withdraw its forces from the portion of Kashmir occupied by it, and its membership of US-sponsored alliances had so altered the regional strategic situation that even the UN mediator Gunnar Jarring was compelled to admit in 1957 that 'the implementation of international agreements of an ad hoc character, which has not been achieved fairly speedily, may become progressively more difficult because the situation with which they were to cope has tended to change'.[8]

The majority of the members of the Security Council allegedly misinterpreted the recommendations of the UN Commission on India and Pakistan (subsequently the UN Representative on India and Pakistan), and the mediators appointed by it, to draft resolutions that India considered partisan, inimical to its interests, and going beyond the scope of the original complaint filed by it. As former Foreign Secretary of India J.N. Dixit wrote:

> The manner in which the United Nations handled the Kashmir issue from 1948 onwards is a dismal story from India's point of view. Instead of taking action on the merits of the issue, on the basis of the constitutional and legal accession of Jammu & Kashmir to India, and instead of asking Pakistan to withdraw from its aggression, the United Nations over the years converted what should have been the issue of 'invasion of Jammu & Kashmir, a part of India, by Pakistan' into 'an India-Pakistan dispute.'. . . . Instead of questioning Pakistan's resort to force for territorial aggrandizement, the UN treated Pakistan on par with India as a disputant on the issue. . . . There was also arrogant indifference on the part of the major powers, both bilaterally and at the UN, about the Kashmir issue. The psychological implication was that newly independent states emerging from colonialism were not capable of managing their political affairs in a rational

[8] Ibid., p. 91.

and practical manner and therefore the issue should be dealt with in a paternal and impartial fashion. . . .[9]

The activities and honesty of the UNMOGIP have also come in for criticism from the Indian side, because:

> despite being on both sides of the ceasefire line, (it) could not stop Pakistan's subversive activities in India right till 1965, after which India rejected the jurisdiction of this group. Not only was this group unable to prevent the subversive activities, even its reports on incidents and situations were obfuscatory and not ready to pin the responsibility on Pakistan.[10]

Indian policy makers believe that even some Pakistanis privately endorse the Indian view of the futility of taking the issue to international forums, and know that it will not lead to conflict resolution. Kuldip Nayar, the well-known Indian journalist, cites Zulfikar Ali Bhutto telling him after giving the commitment to bilateralism in the Simla accord, 'We are not going to activate the UN because what has the UN done? The UN has not done anything much.'[11]

Despite the change in the nature of the international order after the end of bipolarity, the UN today remains as hierarchical an organization as it was at the time of its setting up—controlled by a few powerful states. The reality is that the voices of all the states in respect to its functioning and structure are not being heard fairly and justly. The end of the Cold War has removed the checks and balances in the working of the UN imposed by the bipolar order of the Cold War. American influence over this global organization is even more dominant and controlling today. In these circumstances, there are fears about the neutrality and effectiveness of any UN mediation or involvement in the India–Pakistan conflict.

[9] J.N. Dixit, *India-Pakistan in War and Peace*, New Delhi: Books Today, 2002, pp. 118–20.

[10] J.N. Dixit, 'Making a Case against Multilateral Intervention in Kashmir': http://www.newsindia-times.com/2002/06/28/opinion2.html, 28 June 2002.

[11] Kuldip Nayar, *Distant Neighbours: A Tale of the Subcontinent*, New Delhi: Vikas, 1972, p. 180.

Rejection of the Demand for Plebiscite under UN Supervision

India has been resolutely opposed to plebiscite or any reference to the so-called 'will of the Kashmiri people' for resolving the Kashmir issue. It believes that its acceptance of the proposal made in the resolution of the UN Commission on India and Pakistan of 13 August 1948 (No. S/1100) for a plebiscite cannot hold in the absence of immediate withdrawal of Pakistani forces from the areas occupied by it then. The resolution was very clear that it could be implemented only after the UNCIP was able to satisfy India that Pakistan had taken all the prior steps stipulated in Part IIA and Part IIB of the resolution. These sequential steps had to be taken *first* by Pakistan, and *then* by India. Pakistan had to withdraw all the troops sent in by it, followed by assistance in withdrawal of some five thousand invaders from its North-West Frontier Province. After clearing the territory thus, the rule of the local authorities that prevailed before the accession of the state to India had to be restored under the supervision of the UN. After these steps were taken, India had to withdraw its troops by stages from the areas under its control. Fulfillment of all these conditions was essential before plebiscite in the whole of the former princely state of Jammu & Kashmir. Since none of the initial steps have been taken, the last step of plebiscite cannot be demanded in isolation.

Moreover, the UN resolutions cannot be applicable for eternity. The 1948 resolutions were relevant only in the context of the circumstances prevailing then. In 1957, UN Representative Gunnar Jarring conveyed to the Security Council that the events had so overtaken the resolution of 1948 that it could no longer be implemented.[12]

As the promise for plebiscite was predicated on non-use of force for settling the Kashmir dispute, Pakistan's use of force to wrest Kashmir in 1965 brought to an end any legitimacy of its claim for self-determination. Besides, in contravention of the UN

[12] Pran Chopra, *India, Pakistan and the Kashmir Tangle*, New Delhi: HarperCollins, 1995, p. 64.

resolution, Pakistan incorporated the northern areas of Kashmir under its control into the Pakistani federation. Pakistan has also ceded 2,700 square miles of the territory of Kashmir to China through an agreement in 1963. In addition, China has also occupied a large chunk of territory in Ladakh after its war with India in 1962. The Kashmir dispute has, in this sense, become a tripartite dispute rather than remaining a bilateral one. As a result, the old resolutions of the UN can no longer be considered valid.

Self-determination, the philosophy behind the demand for plebiscite in Kashmir, cannot be applied selectively to some states alone. Such selective application makes self-determination a shield in the hands of some powers for furthering their influence and legitimizing their strategic designs.[13] Even as it appears to be a liberal and democratic option in principle, self-determination is liable to be misused for ulterior purposes, as no universal norms for implementing the principle of self-determination exist. The circumstances under which the right to self-determination should prevail over the sovereign right of nations have not been defined. Hence, the present international system does not support the idea of self-determination, because if this is accepted as the basis of creation of states, the total number of states in the world might be in the range of 1,000–5,000.

PAKISTAN'S POSITION ON INTERNATIONAL MEDIATION

At the negotiations in Simla, the harsh realities of the post-1971 situation compelled Zulfikar Ali Bhutto to accept the Indian condition of bilateralism in future dealings on Kashmir. However, this commitment was interpreted by Pakistan more as an affirmation of its status as a defeated party in the war than as a genuine diplomatic turnaround. Not surprisingly, bilateralism was soon abandoned by Pakistan, which has ever since tried to internationalize the Kashmir problem and sought the involvement of the Western powers in its settlement. Within weeks of the Simla Agreement, Pakistan stated that that accord did not mean Paki-

[13] Ibid., p. 52.

stan agreeing to the withdrawal of UN military observers, or not seeking outside support for its demands. Pakistan's press also argued that commitment to bilateralism did not preclude Pakistan from using other means to draw attention to the Kashmir issue, including using international forums and the UN.[14] All governments that came to power in Pakistan after Zulfikar Ali Bhutto's regime have rejected the Simla Agreement in its letter and spirit, particularly its commitment to bilateralism.

As a weaker party in the conflict and as a state interested in changing the status quo in Jammu & Kashmir, Pakistan has always insisted on and campaigned for mediation and external involvement to pressurize India to respect the UN resolutions on the subject and resolve the problem. Pakistan considers talk of bilateralism as an Indian ploy to steer clear of deliberation on uncomfortable facts and realities of the Kashmir problem and delay its resolution. Capturing the mood of the Pakistani policy makers, President Pervez Musharraf remarked in an interview to the *New York Times*: 'India had squandered several recent opportunities to start serious talks with the Kashmiris and Pakistan.... Unless there is mediation, strong mediation, justice cannot come about.... Mediation is definitely required, and East Timor provides an excellent example of how the situation can be solved if the world community shows the will.'[15] Pakistan has also roped in the Organization of Islamic Conference (OIC) to support its demand for international mediation on Kashmir.[16]

Pakistan believes that India's refusal to admit that there is a dispute relating to Kashmir, and its claim that whatever happens there falls strictly in the domain of internal sovereignty cannot convince anyone about the value of the bilateral approach. Almost the whole world knows Kashmir as a disputed territory and recognizes Pakistan's *locus standi vis-à-vis* the Kashmir problem. By taking the Kashmir dispute to the UN, India *de facto* conceded

[14] Nayar, *Distant Neighbours*, p. 41.

[15] 'Kashmir dispute: CE for East Timor Like Mediation': http://www.dawn.com/2000/09/07/top2.htm, 7 September 2000.

[16] P.S. Suryanarayana, 'Kashmir: OIC for UN Mediation', *The Hindu* (Chennai), 1 July 2000.

the international character of the Kashmir dispute. The provisions of the Simla Agreement also implicitly recognize that there is a dispute relating to Kashmir, and that Pakistan has a right to talk about it with India as well as anywhere else in the world. President Musharraf has termed the Indian position that Kashmir is not an international issue as 'hypocrisy'. He said: 'There is hypocrisy in this attitude. They just juggle around with the semantics of words like mediator, facilitator and interlocutor, but the reality is that Kashmir has already been internationalized.... What are Colin Powell or Jack Straw doing and what are world governments and world powers doing, except talking of Kashmir?'[17]

The key reason for the ineffectiveness of UN mediation on Kashmir in the 1950s was the paralysing influence of the all-out conflict between the American and Soviet blocs on the functioning of this international organization. The UN, India–Pakistan relations and the Kashmir questions were sucked into the power politics of the Cold War. Now that the ideological and strategic divide of the Cold War era is a thing of the past, the probability of success of international mediation on Kashmir has increased, as testified by the increasing involvement of the UN in crisis management and peacekeeping operations.

In today's age, no problem—certainly no problem as grave as Kashmir—can be considered as purely internal and beyond international involvement. Multilateral negotiations are a necessity and a norm in current diplomacy. In the light of the qualitative changes in the international systemic context, new foreign policy responses and participation in multilateral diplomacy have become imperative. Bilateralism of the sort favoured by India is not much in vogue. Few issues and events today remain genuinely bilateral in character. India ought to recognize this reality sooner rather than later. Indeed, India's doctrine of bilateralism is a euphemism for some kind of an Indian version of the Monroe Doctrine.[18]

[17] 'Kashmir Already Inernationalized: Musharraf': http://www.ndtv.com/template/template.asp?id=27704&template=indopakfaceoff&callid=1, 1 August 2002.

[18] Sunanda K. Datta-Ray, 'South Asia: An Indian Version of the Monroe Doctrine', *International Herald Tribune*, 12 April 1989.

In the view of some Pakistani scholars, third-party involvement in Kashmir might also throw up new ideas to solve the problem, which has got bogged down in conflicting interpretations of the disputants. On the Kashmir dispute:

> [T]he bilateral framework moulds into a zero-sum game so there is no room for flexibility. Standard positions are reasserted over and over again while the dispute continues unabated and prevents the creation of a stable South Asian strategic environment. Hence, the need to look beyond the bilateral framework in seeking a format within which a viable solution to the Kashmir issue can be found.[19]

[19] Shireen M. Mazari, 'Kashmir: Choices Before India', *Defence Journal*: http://www.defencejournal.com/sept99/kashmir-choices.htm, September 1999.

CHAPTER 5

Mediation in India–Pakistan Conflict: Potential and Constraints

Antecedent variables—conditions and contingencies under which a particular relationship or phenomenon is most likely to occur—are very significant. Such social, psychological, political and historical variables constitute the overarching context determining the nature and outcomes of a phenomenon. The effectiveness of mediation depends as much upon these contextual factors as on the interests and resources of the parties and the mediator. In the light of antecedent conditions and contextual factors, this chapter evaluates how far India–Pakistan conflict lends itself to resolution through third-party intervention. We shall examine the arguments on the relevance of mediation, then see in what manner these contextual factors help or hinder third-party role in India–Pakistan conflict.

FACTORS FAVOURING INTERNATIONAL MEDIATION

FAILURE OF THE BILATERAL APPROACH

Considering the experience of bilateral negotiations between India and Pakistan in the last three decades, analysts and commentators expect no breakthrough from the pursuit of such contacts. Bilateralism cannot be allowed to become a religion and act as a barrier to conflict management and mitigation, specially when there are no reliable, developed and regular mechanisms of bilateralism between the two states that can be 'counted upon to withstand the sorts of pressures that may be brought against them'.[1] When other methods of conflict management have been tried without success, what is the harm in experimenting with third-party techniques now? After all, mediation rarely does more harm than good.[2] Even if it does not result in any agreement, such an effort can at least help improve understanding of each others' perspectives. Besides, if any India–Pakistan accord has to work, it will require international guarantees. Bilateral accords like the Simla Agreement failed due to the lack of such guarantees, which can be obtained only if international actors join in the negotiation and settlement processes.[3]

Introduction of Nuclear Weapons in South Asia

In open defiance of global pressure, and abandoning their own earlier protestations of the peaceful use of nuclear energy and commitment to nuclear disarmament, India and Pakistan detonated multiple nuclear devices at Pokhran and Chagai, respectively, in May 1998 to gatecrash into the exclusive nuclear club. The two countries have also acquired delivery systems in the form of short- and medium-range missiles to make their nuclear capability strategically relevant.

Nuclear weapons present the gravest danger to global security today. The short flight time of ballistic missiles between India and Pakistan raises the level of concern and risk associated with nuclear weapons. It will be simplistic to assume that with the testing of nuclear capability by India and Pakistan, nuclear deterrence will prevail automatically between them. It is often doubted whether India and Pakistan have the necessary technical and scientific skills to manage a nuclear arsenal safely, and operate a sophisticated command, control and communication system for the strategic

[1] Robert G. Wirsing, *India, Pakistan and the Kashmir Dispute: On Regional Conflict and its Resolution*, New York: St. Martin's Press, 1994, p. 249.

[2] Jacob Bercovitch, 'The Structure and Diversity of Mediation in International Relations', in Jacob Bercovitch and Jeffrey Rubin (eds.), *Mediation in International Relations*, New York: St. Martin's Press, 1992, pp. 9–10.

[3] Shekhar Gupta, 'Junk the Scripture of Bilateralism', *Indian Express* (New Delhi), 9 December 2000.

forces. Suspicions are also raised about the safety of the nuclear weapons and materials in Pakistan. Some experts apprehend that 'the danger of catastrophic system accidents involving complex technologies in India and Pakistan remains particularly high'.[4]

Sustained dialogue is, therefore, required to minimize the possibility of use or threat of use of nuclear weapons, stabilize nuclear deterrent postures through suitable arms control measures, work on contingency and crisis management scenarios, lower the incentives to start a conventional war, and structure an elaborate command and control system that puts brakes on the use of nuclear weapons due to accident or miscalculation. In the memorandum of understanding accompanying the Lahore Declaration of February 1999 and signed by the foreign secretaries of the two states, India and Pakistan had decided to notify each other immediately in the event of any accidental, unexplained or unauthorized incident that could create the risk of nuclear war. They had also agreed to maintain a unilateral moratorium on further nuclear tests, conclude an agreement to prevent incidents at sea, upgrade and improve the existing communication links with a view to making them compatible with the dangers of accidental nuclear exchange, and engage in bilateral consultations on security, disarmament and non-proliferation issues. However, this expression of intent could not be converted into a treaty arrangement due to the subsequent deterioration in bilateral relations.

Hence, the efforts of the international community will be increasingly focussed on ensuring 'nuclear peace' in South Asia and preventing a nuclear arms race. The big powers will not wait for the resolution of the contentious disputes between India and Pakistan to press for nuclear risk reduction measures (NRRM) between them. Irrespective of the progress on other fronts of their relationship, India and Pakistan would have to address and accommodate the concerns of the international community to work for nuclear risk reduction. Mediation by political actors, tech-

[4] Tariq Rauf, 'Nuclear and Missile CBMs in South Asia', in Dipankar Banerji (ed.), *Confidence Building Measures in South Asia*, Colombo: Regional Centre for Strategic Studies, 1999, p. 135.

nical and strategic experts, economists and non-governmental organizations of the five nuclear powers could prove useful in achieving this goal.

International Ramifications of India–Pakistan Conflict

An intimate link exists between the international systemic environment and the conduct of relations between states. This link cannot be wished away, more so in the present complex, interdependent and interpenetrated world. As a distinct international subsystem, South Asia is a region of considerable strategic importance for the Western powers. Maintenance of strategic stability in South Asia is significant from the commercial, political and military points of view. Moreover, the nuclear explosions at Pokhran and Chagai in May 1998 have irreversibly internationalized the India–Pakistan conflict and the Kashmir issue. In the post-nuclear era, Kashmir is being perceived as the most dangerous place on earth and a potential nuclear flashpoint. If India expects the rest of the world not to take interest in the ups and downs of its relations with Pakistan, it is divorced from the reality of world politics. It is, therefore, no longer possible for India and Pakistan to conduct their relations unaffected by the interests and propositions of the dominant coalition of powers. Formal or informal mediation by this coalition is inescapable in the event of a serious break in their relations. The emerging realities of South Asia's interstate politics in the era of globalization and increasing interdependence of states should, therefore, persuade India's policy makers to review their insistence on bilateralism.

Mediation is a Fait Accompli

Notwithstanding what the Indian representatives might say, there is increasing receptiveness to third-party intervention and facilitation among policy makers and strategic commentators in South Asia. Despite their commitment to bilateralism, 'India and Pakistan have willy-nilly allowed the US the role of an arbiter in bilateral relations in the last two years. From Musharraf's televised addresses to his promises, from Atalji's friendship initiatives to his coercive diplomacy, Washington has been the implicit addressee as well as the court of final appeal for both parties.'[5]

India's concerted attempts and eagerness to solicit international support against Pakistan for providing material, logistical and political support to the terrorists operating in the valley of Kashmir disagree with its declared policy of addressing the conflict in a bilateral framework and not drawing in the world community. Such lobbying against Pakistan legitimizes Pakistan's attempts to internationalize the Kashmir issue.[6]

India is not Unreceptive to International Mediation in Principle

Even as India opposes third-party role in its conflict with Pakistan, it is a fact that India itself has acted as mediator or facilitator in disputes involving other states, and it is not averse to the principle of international mediation in general. The Directive Principles of the Indian Constitution enjoin the Government of India to 'encourage settlement of international disputes by arbitration'. India played a successful mediatory role in the UN-sponsored efforts to settle the problem of the repatriation of 1,40,000 Chinese prisoners of war towards the end of the Korean War in the 1950s. The Indian formula was accepted by all the parties—North Korea, South Korea, and China. India also acted as a mediator during the 1954 UN conference on Indo-China held at Geneva. Its good offices were used in initiating negotiations between the Government of Sri Lanka and the LTTE in the 1980s. All this makes the Indian stance on mediation in the India–Pakistan conflict seem paradoxical and illogical. In the words of one Indian expert, 'to have mediated but to refuse mediation is illogical behaviour'.[7]

[5] Editorial, *Times of India* (Ahmedabad), 16 May 2003.

[6] Sushil J. Aaron, 'Jettisoning Bilateralism: Is India Ready for a Madrid Conference?', article no. 215: http://www.ipcs.org/ipcs/issueIndex2.jsp?action=showView&kValue=525&issue=1011&status=article&mod=b, 29 June 1999.

[7] P. R. Chari, 'The Mantra of Bilateralism', article no. 220: http://www.ipcs.org/ipcs/issueIndex2.jsp?action=showView&kValue=513&issue=1011&status=article&mod=b, 9 July 1999.

Mediation can Break the Deadlock in Negotiations

Ideally, the parties involved in a dispute should settle their own conflict because they have created it in the first place, and they have the maximum stake in its resolution. However, as Edward de Bono writes:

> ... the parties involved in a conflict may actually be in the worst position to resolve their conflict—except where the outcome is to be determined by force.... It is the logic of the situation and it could not be otherwise ... the very involvement of the parties and the fact that they have much to gain or to lose makes them incapable of providing all the thinking needed for resolution of the conflict.[8]

Direct negotiations between adversaries can also accentuate the power disparity between them and intensify their confrontation. A third party is able to take a dispassionate and unprejudiced view of the situation, and provide the broader context within which the conflict can be resolved.

Because of the structure of their conflict, and lack of trust and communication between them, India and Pakistan are bogged down in an argumentative mode of thinking and are unable to cultivate the creative and problem-solving attitude required for the settlement of their conflict. They have seldom conducted substantive dialogue on the actual nitty-gritty of differences between them. Stephen Cohen writes that:

> [M]eetings between Indians and Pakistanis rarely last long enough to systematically discuss the differences between the two sides and how those differences might be ameliorated or accommodated. Any discussion on the strategic and structural problem of a large India working out its differences with smaller neighbours is likely, sooner or later, to move upward to a discussion of civilizational differences (presumably incompatible ones) or downward to personality differences or the intractability of certain issues (nuclear proliferation, trade, water and so forth), or laterally to the responsibility of outside powers for regional disputes.[9]

[8] Edward de Bono, *Conflicts: A Better Way to Resolve Them*, London: Penguin, 1991, p. 100.

[9] Stephen P. Cohen, *The Structural Dimensions of Conflict in South Asia*, Colombo: Regional Centre for Strategic Studies, 1997, p. 11.

Both countries have rich experience in the conduct of international diplomacy, as proven by their record in various international organizations and multilateral forums. The services of Indian and Pakistani diplomats have also been hired by the UN for its peacemaking efforts. However, when it comes to the management of their own conflict, such diplomatic experience has proven ineffective in taking bilateral negotiations in a positive direction. The presence of a mediator and his assistance in negotiations can prove helpful in resolving the logjam that often bedevils India–Pakistan bilateral talks.

Mediation Provides Choice to the Parties

Mediation offers an element of choice to the disputing parties from the beginning till the end. It is generally the most acceptable of third-party techniques since, unlike arbitration or adjudication, the disputants are not obligated to accept the views of the mediator. Their commitment to the mediation process is purely voluntary. They also retain high control over the process and outcomes of mediation. Mediation provides a choice to the parties to decide whom to select as a mediator, what procedures to follow, the extent of mediator involvement, how much concession they want to give to the other party and so on. Parties have ample opportunity to present their points of view, information and ideas, and also have the option of rejecting the outcome of mediation if they wish.

Neutral Mediators may not be Imperative

One of India's arguments against mediation is that it is not easy to find impartial mediators among states and international organizations which use mediation to advance their own interests and agenda. While impartiality and evenhandedness are desirable attributes in mediation, they are not an absolute must. Even partial mediators can achieve success if they have sufficient leverage with one or both the parties. The US tilt towards Israel in its conflict with the Arab states is well known to all the participants in the Middle East conflict. Yet it could act as a mediator in this conflict, and succeeded in concluding some agreements.

CONSTRAINTS ON MEDIATION

The Issues of India–Pakistan Conflict are not Amenable to Mediation

When the interests of two parties are not fundamentally divergent, and the issues of the conflict revolve around the means of achieving the same goals, it is easier to convince them about the need for an agreement. However, if the parties hold zero-sum and mutually exclusive positions on their national identity and security, no amount of third-party activity is likely to bear positive results. As R.F. Randel argues, 'should a dispute affect vital security interests of the parties, no amount of mediation by a third party is likely to prevent the outbreak of hostilities'.[10] The failure of the PLO–Israel agreements of 1993 and 1995 to ensure peace and stability in the region is an illustration of the ineffectiveness of mediated and imposed outcomes in conflicts involving territory and issues of identity, nationalism, justice and sovereignty. Such issues are non-negotiable, and do not lend themselves to accord even when the costs of continuing the hostilities are high, and when there is no possibility of an outright victory of any one party.

Most of the disputes between India and Pakistan involve conflicting claims over territories (Jammu & Kashmir, Siachen Glacier, Sir Creek, among others) that the two countries consider to be economically or strategically vital. Mutual adjustment of minor territorial claims of the parties is possible through third-party techniques like arbitration or mediation, but when territories are so large (as Jammu & Kashmir) or important, such techniques are rendered ineffective because 'it is one of the principles of negotiations that when territory is at stake, the party in possession tends to resist third party involvement'.[11]

[10] R.F. Randel, *The Origins of Peace*, New York: Free Press, 1973, p. 49.

[11] A. Lall, *Modern International Negotiation*, New York: Columbia University Press, 1966, p. 100.

The Nature of India–Pakistan Conflict

Intractable and high-intensity conflicts cannot be easily subjected to mediation or other forms of third-party intervention. The India–Pakistan conflict is not just a traditional interstate conflict over a piece of land. The causes of this conflict are deeply entrenched in the history, popular psyche, and societies of the two states. Had it not been so, the conflict would have been resolved by now. The India–Pakistan conflict is also heavily influenced by the real or perceived national identities of the two states. Conflicts of identity are different from the more straightforward wars over territory, resources, or power. As identities are indivisible, such conflicts become very complex and intractable, much less amenable to compromise, negotiation, or trade-off.

Few other international conflicts are as profoundly influenced by historical memories, events and determinants as the India–Pakistan conflict. The history of the last one millennium casts a shadow over today's political and strategic issues. The conflict is the carry-over of a historical struggle, with political and strategic issues providing a ruse to accelerate it further. Historical memories—rather, reconstructed and fantastic history—provides the backdrop to India–Pakistan relations.[12] Such reconstructed history is used for satisfying contemporary and future purposes. The developments and recollections of the Partition of 1947, as well as Pakistan's memories of the defeat in the war for the liberation of Bangladesh in 1971, make it extremely difficult to apply conflict resolving mechanisms between these two States.

The India–Pakistan conflict bears many features of a conflict between civilizations for survival and expansion. India and Pakistan use cultural and civilization-related parameters to define themselves and their identities. Each state emphasizes the characteristics (tradition, customs, heritage, literature, religion, language, values, norms) that presumably distinguish itself from the other. Each state looks upon itself as a distinctive and superior civiliza-

[12] Asish Nandy, 'The Fantastic India-Pakistan Battle', *Futures*, vol. 29, no. 10, 1997, p. 909.

tion. The threat from the other is perceived not just in military or territorial terms, but also as a threat to its civilization. The quest for security is aimed at preserving one's civilization against the expansionist and demonic intents of the other's civilization. Such imagery of a conflict of civilizations is accentuated by selective historical memories and ideological understandings invoked to demonize the other. The popular discourse on India–Pakistan conflict has many similarities to the impending 'clash of civilizations' propounded in a book of the same title by Samuel Huntington.

The psychological factors also exercise a profound influence on international conflicts. The individual and collective psychological process mediates much of the behaviour of the states.[13] Ultimately, it is the attitudes and perceptions of conflicting parties that influence their negotiating stance as well as actual negotiations, and expand or reduce the bargaining space available to them. The conflict between India and Pakistan is also rendered intractable because of the psychological structure of the conflict, and interaction of this structure with the political, historical and strategic factors. The way this conflict and its causes are internalized, interpreted and psychologically processed by the Indian and Pakistani societies has profound influence on the course of the conflict itself. The opening statement of the preamble of UNESCO's charter ('Since war begins in the minds of men, it is in the minds of men that defenses of peace must be erected') might be applicable most to India and Pakistan. The India–Pakistan conflict is a state of mind. While it is apparently manifested territorially and strategically, it is primarily a psychological conflict. Such conflicts are difficult to manage, mediate, and resolve.

Describing the psychological structure of this relationship as a 'paired minority conflict', Stephen Cohen writes:

[13] Herbert C. Kelman, 'Social Psychological Dimensions of International Conflict', in I. William Zartman and J. Lewis Rasmussen (eds.), *Peacemaking in International Conflict: Methods and Techniques*, Washington: United States Institute of Peace Press, 1997, p. 192.

> [E]ach side in these paired structures sees itself as a minority, or a weaker state, facing the more powerful entity. In such conflicts, it is extraordinarily difficult for one side to offer reassuring concessions or agree to compromise on even trivial issues. To do so is seen as confirming others' perceptions of one's own weakness and to invite further demands. . . . [These conflicts] seem to be able to draw on an inexhaustible supply of hatred towards the other side and distrust of advocates of dialogue or compromise.[14]

In this conflict, both parties perceive themselves as a persecuted minority, victimized and vulnerable.[15] Both highlight, for their respective purposes, the fear of attack from a more powerful and aggressive neighbour.

Most societies need enemies for sustenance. If they do not have any, one is invented. This is considered necessary for maintaining the unity of the group and making the society conscious of the importance of this unity.[16] India and Pakistan also feel the necessity for an enemy in each other. Both have developed largely positive images of themselves and negative images of the other. Violence and aggression become associated with the other party, while virtue and justice are believed to be on one's own side. Such a situation, in which one side perceives itself as only good and the other side as only evil, can lead to a self-fulfilling prophecy, and eruption of violence. Such irrational enemy mythology has also locked India and Pakistan in a zero-sum conflict. India's gain is considered a loss for Pakistan, and vice versa. The opportunities to weaken the other in all possible ways or show one-upmanship are always welcome.

The Kashmir Problem: A Cul-de-Sac

Most people would want to remember Kashmir as a picturesque territory tucked away in the Himalaya in the northern extreme of India. However, the events of the last five decades and unre-

[14] Ibid.

[15] Cohen, *Structural Dimensions of Conflict*, p. 1.

[16] G. Simmel, *Conflict and the Web of Group Affiliations*, New York: Free Press, 1955, p. 98.

lenting terrorism in the region have transformed this 'paradise on earth' into a 'nuclear flashpoint' and the 'most dangerous place on earth'. With the beginning of the present spell of terrorism from 1989, Kashmir is in the news almost daily, not so much for its breathtaking beauty, but for some of the most brutal acts of violence and vandalism by the militants. Despite the Indian government's claims to the contrary, militancy in the Kashmir Valley refuses to die or abate. According to estimates, about 50,000 persons, including a large number of security personnel, have lost their lives in the terrorist violence in the last decade.[17] The terrorist violence, which was initially restricted to the Valley region, has also spread to Jammu and Ladakh. Terrorist outfits like the Lashkar-e-Toiba, Harkat-ul-Ansar and Hizbul Mujahideen have adopted the strategy of expanding their theatre of war outside the state to New Delhi, Mumbai, and other metropolitan cities.

Kashmir is more than just another interstate territorial dispute. It is a key determinant of the competing visions of nationalism of India and Pakistan. More importantly, it is about the legitimacy of the models of nation building adopted by the two states. The multiple imponderables and variables impinging on the situation in Kashmir make it extremely complex and unpredictable. It has rightly been called the 'Jerusalem of South Asia'—a seemingly intractable problem.[18] With thousands of soldiers and weapons on both sides of the LOC, Kashmir is one of the most heavily militarized areas of the world. The prospects of stability and peace in the region depend critically upon events in Kashmir.

The roots of the Kashmir conflict lie in the differing interpretations of the basis of Partition by India and Pakistan. Pakistan claims that since religion was the basis of the division of colonial India, a Muslim-majority province like Kashmir should have joined Pakistan as a matter of natural course. Both the legality and morality of Kashmir's accession to India are rejected by Pakistan. India, on the other hand, argues that the accession of Kashmir to

[17] For detailed information about the acts of terrorist violence in Jammu & Kashmir in recent times, see: www.satp.org

[18] Cohen, *Structural Dimensions of Conflict*, p. 13.

India was arrived at through politically, legally and morally valid methods. Pakistan is actually the guilty party in Kashmir, having occupied 34,000 square miles out of the total of 84,471 square miles of the territory of the erstwhile princely state of Jammu & Kashmir through aggression. This includes about 17,000 square miles of Gilgit, about 12,000 square miles of Baltistan, and about 5,000 square miles of the Mirpur–Poonch–Muzaffarabad sector.

Kashmir is the bedrock of India's constitutive principles of secularism, pluralism, and democracy. India has argued that its nationalism does not rest on the assertion of any one ethnicity, religion, or linguistic group, but transcends and amalgamates all of them. There is ample scope for the expression of all legitimate identities within the Indian union. Reopening the issue of the accession of Kashmir to the Indian union is tantamount to rejection of this ideological core of the Indian republic. Consisting of various religious groups (Hindus, Muslims, Buddhists and Sikhs), the state of Jammu & Kashmir itself is a microcosm of the larger pluralistic and multi-religious ethos of India.

Kashmir as an integral part of India has great political and ideological significance. Revision of the accession of Kashmir for being a Muslim-majority state would not only negate all that the Indian state has stood for and withheld, but also set off similar demands from other religious and ethnic groups not merely in India, but across South Asia, and cause anarchy in the region. Secessionism by the various tribal insurgency groups in northeast India, Tamils in Sri Lanka, or Baluchis, Sindhis and Pashtuns in Pakistan, would acquire new vigour if nationalist concessions were granted on the strength of ethnic or religious identities.

Pakistan feels an intense emotional and religious attachment to Kashmir. It regards the integration of the state of Jammu & Kashmir as 'an unfinished agenda' of Partition. Until this Muslim-majority region becomes part of Pakistan, Partition will remain incomplete. If the states of Bhopal, Hyderabad, and Junagadh with Muslim rulers and Hindu-majority populations acceded to India, it was logical for the state of Jammu & Kashmir with a Muslim-majority population and a Hindu ruler to accede to Pakistan. Control over Kashmir would also give Pakistan secure access to China and the Central Asian Republics, apart from putting it in a strategically strong position *vis-à-vis* north and northwestern India. Since all the major rivers flowing through Pakistani Punjab originate from Kashmir, Pakistan has economic and strategic interests in the state. It apprehends that 'India, being in control of Jammu & Kashmir, can create geological and economic chaos for it by simply manipulating the headwaters of the rivers within Kashmir territory according to its political and strategic interests.'[19] Former Pakistan President Ayub Khan once stated:

> ...just look at the map of Kashmir. Just look at the location of rivers on which the life of whole of West Pakistan, of some 45 million people depends. As our population increases, every drop of water has to be husbanded, stored and utilized. Then there is the added problem of our security, of physical and military security. The present ceasefire line is just like a grip around our neck.[20]

Kashmir is a unique international problem in view of its association with territorial claims, religious consciousness, ethnic identities, domestic factors, and international interests. However, it apparently shares several common features with other ethnic secessionist movements like the ones in East Timor (when it was a part of Indonesia), Sri Lanka, Northern Ireland in the UK, Bosnia and Kosovo in Yugoslavia, or Chechnya in Russia. The international community recognizes these commonalities. Its line of thinking on Kashmir will, therefore, be influenced by its approach to other ethnic conflicts.

Even as it seems extremely unlikely to get the UN involved in Kashmir given its stated disinclination to play any role in this conflict, a suggestion has been made to formalize a standstill agreement between India and Pakistan and place the territory of Jammu & Kashmir under the direct control of the UN as a trusteeship territory. After a gap of an agreed-upon period (10 or 20 years), a

[19] Ibid., p. 204.

[20] Quoted by Rais Ahmad Jafri, *Ayub: Soldier and Statesman*, Lahore: Mohammad Ali Academy, 1966, p. 156.

plebiscite can be held to determine the wishes of the people. Placing Kashmir as a UN trusteeship territory has an intrinsic appeal. It will 'remove the state's internal crisis, defuse a militarily dangerous situation on its external border with Pakistan, and... supply a neutral institutional mechanism to preside over a peaceful and unhurried search for a permanent settlement'.[21]

The success or failure of international mediation stops at the door of Kashmir. Scholars and commentators have been at their wits' end trying to discover the magic formula that would solve the Kashmir problem. It would be rash and irrational to suggest instant formulae as solutions for Kashmir. The multiple imponderables and variables impinging on the situation in Kashmir make it extremely complex and unpredictable. Pakistan's nothing-except-Kashmir, and India's everything-but-Kashmir stands are unlikely to produce any results for some time to come. Indeed, conflict resolution in Kashmir cannot be consciously attempted. It could only emerge from a long-drawn-out process in which changes of perceptions of the two sides precede the application of concrete steps for peace. This process of perceptual changes will consist of several interconnected measures between India and Pakistan in the economic, political, and psychological spheres.

The question as to how far mediation could succeed in building confidence between India and Pakistan on the Kashmir problem, and how far Kashmir frustrates mediation efforts does not have a conclusive answer. Third parties can play only a symbolic role in conflicts where the political and economic benefits of conflict settlement appear far less significant than the social and psychological benefits of persisting with the conflict. Even the celebrated international mediator and former US Secretary of State Henry L. Kissinger acknowledged that the Kashmir issue was not fit for international mediation because it involved competing perceptions of the two nations about their nationhood.[22]

[21] Wirsing, *India, Pakistan and the Kashmir Dispute*, p. 223.

[22] 'Kashmir Not Fit Case for Mediation', *Statesman* (Kolkata), 6 June 2002.

He emphasized that no country, not even the only superpower America, could impose any solution on India and Pakistan.[23]

It seems certain, therefore, that neither India nor Pakistan would abandon their historical and ideological claims on Kashmir due to a mediator's pressure or incentives. For India, inviting a third party in the Kashmir negotiations will indirectly provide legitimacy to Pakistan's claims on Kashmir, which it considers unacceptable. The two states should not be expected by the international community to agree to an impractical solution, or immediately give up claims they have held for decades without matching quid pro quos. Any possible solution of the Kashmir dispute should also give satisfaction to the two countries for their diplomatic and military efforts for retaining or securing Kashmir.

A Mix of Domestic and Interstate Conflict

That the India–Pakistan conflict is not purely an interstate conflict, but has strong domestic roots and consequences, is another reason why mediation might not be so relevant for resolving it. Few other interstate relationships are as critically affected by internal factors and popular sentiments. This conflict is deeply entrenched in the societal level of the two states. The critical role of domestic and sub-national factors differentiates the India–Pakistan conflict from other conflicts. In this sense, it is an interpenetrated conflict with a certain 'transnational' character. The intermeshing of interstate and intrastate conflicts complicates the strategic situation in South Asia, and makes application of mediation difficult.

Mediation in an intractable conflict is likely to be successful when each party has strong and recognized leaders enjoying legitimacy in the dominant sections of their societies and exercising control over popular attitudes. When the leaders are weak and do not command popular acceptance, chances of successful mediation decline sharply. The negotiators and mediators in India–Pakistan relations have to worry constantly about the compulsions of domestic politics, and the support that the leaders

[23] Ibid.

enjoy internally. Even if a mediator is in a position to influence the behaviour of the negotiators, it may not be able to move into the domestic jurisdiction and control the internal constituencies and actors which are hostile to the prospects of peace between the two countries. The constraints of managing coalitions in India, and of keeping the generals of the Pakistan Army satisfied restrict the diplomatic choices and room for manoeuvre available to the Indian and Pakistani leaderships.

The politicians, political parties and the people in power in the Indian subcontinent never like to be perceived as being soft towards the other side. Such a perception can cost them dearly in an election. An aggressive stand towards the neighbour is likely to bring popularity and electoral rewards. As the issues of India–Pakistan relations are very emotive, ballot boxes can be filled up by playing upon the fear of the enemy and exaggerating the threat from across the border. An analysis of the campaign speeches of Indian and Pakistani politicians would reveal how easily complex bilateral strategic matters could fall prey to populist demagoguery.

Upon assumption of power, every Indian and Pakistani ruler tries to project himself as different from his predecessors—peace-loving and rational. However, the compulsions of populist politics soon take the better of his supposed pacifism and push him towards an inflexible stance with the adversary. Deft use of such fears can even help cover up failures of the government in the welfare sector. Governments, therefore, at times generate artificial insecurities to divert attention from their failures. Threats of external attack are also kept alive to legitimize repressive laws and policies, violation of human rights, or higher allocations for the armed forces.

Peacemaking and mediation become ineffective if sections of the society are committed to the continuation of violence. Such sections which believe that their opponent deserves extinction cannot accept the idea of peaceful coexistence. They are the spoilers of the peace process, who have much to lose from peaceful outcome of a conflict, and much to gain from the continuation of violence. The activities of such groups constitute a major obstacle to any mediation effort. There are a number of constituencies resisting the very ideas of confidence building, peace, and a stable relationship between India and Pakistan. Offence for them is the best defence. Such groups are more organized and powerful than the groups committed to peace and normalcy between the two countries.

Religious fundamentalist groups are a major obstacle to peace building efforts all over the world. Recent years have witnessed a steep rise of fundamentalism in both India and Pakistan. The fundamentalists of both countries are each others' mirror images—rigid, uncompromising, mouthing communal hostility, and projecting their own religion and nation as superior to the others'. These forces interpret India–Pakistan relations as determined by the religious identity of the two states. Even as decision makers of the two countries might be guided by hard-nosed strategic realism in formulating their policies, India–Pakistan conflict sometimes assumes the proportions of a *jihad* or a *dharma yuddha* (religious, or righteous war)—an extension of the millennium-old historical conflict between Hindus and Muslims—in popular perception. Fundamentalist groups oppose the opening up of relations in the economic, cultural and social spheres as they fear that such proximity could distract attention from the 'core issues' of the conflict, namely Kashmir and avenging the defeat of 1971 for the Pakistani militant groups, and Pakistani complicity in cross-border terrorism and the larger threat of Islamic fundamentalism to the 'Hindu nation' for the Indian fundamentalist groups. For these groups, exertions to normalize the relations and have a dialogue between the two adversaries are worthless unless the issues of cross-border terrorism or Kashmir are resolved.

Lack of Trust between India and Pakistan

In an anarchic world devoid of supranational authority structures, a state normally imagines and anticipates the worst intentions and behaviour on the part of its adversary. Any unexplained action of the adversary is interpreted as hostile, compelling it to undertake countermeasures to ward off perceived or real threat from the enemy. Such countermeasures in turn generate further hostility and adverse activity in the other state. An endless cycle of insecurity and preparation for security begins. This action-reaction cycle is largely a result of lack of trust or confidence, inadequate or no communication among adversaries, and misperception or negative perception about the 'enemy'.

Mutual confidence is essential for reducing the likelihood of conflict and applying conflict management and resolution techniques. Misunderstanding, mistrust, or misperception are basic causes of the aggravation of a conflict. When the conflicting states are mired in deep distrust and animosity, when they regard their differences as irreconciliable, or when any one state has an incentive to strike first, it is hard for the third party to inspire confidence in the mediator as well as between themselves. This lack of trust acts as an obstacle to conflict resolution and pursuit of negotiations as a means to achieving an optimum outcome of the conflict.

The level of trust between India and Pakistan has sunk so low that it is extremely difficult for external actors to get negotiations going in the desired direction. Recently, India's trust in Pakistan was shattered due to cross-border terrorism in Jammu & Kashmir. India has charged Pakistan with using terrorism as an instrument of state policy, and recruiting, arming, training and financing terrorists and foreign mercenaries who perpetrate acts of violence against the Indian security forces and civilians. The Indian government claims to have documented material evidence of Pakistan's complicity in terrorism. What Pakistan claims as diplomatic, moral and political support to the Kashmir movement, is, in fact, a cover-up for collusion with the Kashmiri militant movement in the form of indoctrination, training, supply of arms and ammunition, and financing.

Pakistan believes, as pointed out by its President Pervez Musharraf, that violence in Kashmir is a result of indigenous protest by the Kashmiri masses against the policies of the Indian government. No outside state, however powerful, could sustain a movement of such scale and intensity for so long against the wishes of the people. According to the Pakistan government, the failure of the Indian government to crush the Kashmiri movement despite the use of military power indicates the strength and indigenous character of this movement.[24]

Mediation is Inapplicable to States with High Capability

Successful international mediation has been applied mostly between such states whose capabilities are low, and which are politically and diplomatically dependent upon external help.[25] Both India and Pakistan are nuclear powers and big states. India is also a major regional power with a large economy and the second-largest population in the world. Can India and Pakistan be considered in the category of states like Cambodia, Namibia or Bolivia that could accept unwelcome settlements due to pressure or economic benefits promised by mediating powers?

Asymmetrical Conflicts Cannot be Resolved Through Third-party Role

Several studies have brought out that mediation is most effective in disputes involving states with equal power. When the parties possess asymmetrical power, their conflict is not apt for resolution through third-party involvement.[26] The greater the power disparity, the lesser the chance of success of mediation. The party that feels more powerful than the other is generally not ready to offer concessions that are essential for a stable agreement. As the data in Tables 5.1 and 5.2 indicate, there is a marked disparity in the levels of military power between India and Pakistan. Both in conventional and nuclear weaponry, India claims numerical and

[24] 'Musharraf Calls for Mediation, Bilateralism on Kashmir has Failed', *Dawn*: http://dawn.com/2002/02/06/top2.htm, 6 February 2002.

[25] Jacob Bercovitch, 'International Mediation and Dispute Settlement: Evaluating the Conditions for Successful Mediation', *Negotiation Journal*, 1991, reproduced in the USIS Special Feature Service article 110, p. 9.

[26] O.R. Young, *The Intermediaries: Third Parties in International Crises*, Princeton: Princeton University Press, 1967; M.C. Ott, 'Mediation as a Method of Conflict Resolution', *International Organization*, vol. 26, pp. 595–618; and Bercovitch, 'International Mediation and Dispute Settlement', pp. 1–27.

TABLE 5.1: COMPARATIVE DATA ON MILITARY CAPABILITIES OF INDIA AND PAKISTAN

	India	Pakistan
Nuclear weapons (est.)	75–100	25–50
Army manpower	11,00,000	5,50,000
Tanks	3,454	2,285
Towed artillery	4,175	1,417
Air Force manpower	1,40,000	40,000
Combat aircraft	730	353
Attack helicopters	32	0
Navy manpower	55,000	22,000
Aircraft carriers	1	0
Submarines	19	10
Destroyers	8	7
Frigates	9	8
Paramilitary forces	10,89,700	2,88,000
Highest missile range	2,000 km	1,500 km

Source: India Today, 27 May and 3 June 2002; *Time*, 14 January 2002.

TABLE 5.2: COMPARATIVE DATA ON ECONOMIC CAPABILITIES OF INDIA AND PAKISTAN (2002)

	India	Pakistan
Gross national income	US $480.8 billion	US $60.9 billion
Per capita gross national income	US $470	US $420
Gross domestic product	US $481.4 billion	US $59.1 billion
Total exports	US $44,915 million	US $9,140 million
Total imports	US $57,618 million	US $9,432 million
Total debt outstanding and disbursed	US $97,071 million	US $35,113 million

Source: http://www.worldbank.org/data/countrydata

qualitative superiority. India also enjoys huge economic superiority over Pakistan. This intrinsic unevenness of power between India and Pakistan engenders conditions of instability and constrains any mediatory initiative. Indeed, there has never been any parity or balance between India and Pakistan. During the Cold

War, an artificial balance of power was being sought to be created by the Western alliance by pumping in large quantities of military and economic aid to Pakistan in return for Pakistani support in the anti-communist agenda. Western support also created a mistaken impression at international platforms that India and Pakistan were equal states.

Rajesh Rajgopalan, applying the structural realist theory to India–Pakistan conflict, has also argued that Pakistan's conflict with India is a consequence of the structure of imbalance of power in South Asia. In his view:

> The India-Pakistan conflict is the direct consequence of the imbalance of power between the two states, and Pakistan's insecurity about this imbalance... and (its) attempts to correct it. The structure of the international system in South Asia has constrained the choices available to India and Pakistan in their relations with each other... since the source of the India-Pakistan conflict is in the natural imbalance of power between India and Pakistan, the solution requires either some change in this imbalance or a change towards bandwagoning in Pakistan's strategy. As long as no such change takes place, Pakistan is likely to continue to be insecure, and the consequence of this insecurity will be continuing India–Pakistan conflict.[27]

One of the reasons for Pakistan's insecurity is its geographic location. About half of its land frontiers are with India, all of which are not protected by any natural barriers. The difference in the territorial sizes of India and Pakistan also exacerbates its insecurity. Pakistan lacks depth in terms of defence. Karachi, its only major port, falls within easy reach of Indian military aircraft. Most of its important towns and industrial establishments lie within 150 miles of Indian territory. Such lack of strategic depth forced Pakistan to look for support from the Western powers, China, and the Middle East during its wars with India in order to make up for the shortcomings in defensive capability and to reduce India's relative power. In the changed post-Cold War scenario, Pakistan can no longer expect promise of open military support from any alliance or state.

[27] Rajesh Rajgopalan, 'Neo-Realist Theory and the India-Pakistan Conflict', *Strategic Analysis*, vol. XXII, no. 9, pp. 1261–72, 1998.

Lack of Agreement on the Agenda of Negotiations

Mediation means *assisted negotiations*. However, when there is a basic divergence in the Indian and Pakistani approaches on the agenda of negotiations, the presence of a mediator in such negotiations is unlikely to make much impact. India believes that Kashmir is just one of the many issues between the two countries. Hence, it prefers a multi-track, composite dialogue covering a wide range of bilateral issues that include, apart from the Kashmir problem, Sir Creek, Siachen Glacier, development of economic and commercial relations, Nuclear Risk Reduction Measures (NRRM), confidence building measures, terrorism, drug trafficking, and so on. Pakistan, on the other hand, argues that Kashmir is the 'core issue', whose resolution alone can normalize relations between the two states. It thus wants that the dialogue be focussed primarily on the Kashmir problem. Once this issue is tackled, progress on other items suggested by India can be made.

Lack of Political Will

As waging peace is far more difficult than waging war, mediation can be applied only if it is backed by strong political will of the disputants and the mediator. The disputants' motivation to control their conflict peacefully and accept third-party role for this purpose is the first requirement for the initiation of mediation. Only when a state is ready to talk and settle with the other side, instead of defeating it, will it consider mediation and negotiation. In the case of India and Pakistan, the basic political will to negotiate and settle differences is conspicuous by its absence. In fact, willingness to talk to the other side is often interpreted as a sign of weakness.

No External Actor Enjoys Coercive Power over India and Pakistan

Outcomes of mediation are determined by the distribution of power between disputants, as well as between mediator and disputants. Though mediation is different from arbitration in the sense that it does not involve authoritative decision making, it is also true that without the use of coercive power, the mediator may not be able to deliver a positive outcome. Mediation succeeds when an external actor has controlling influence over the conflicting parties. Success of third-party mediation in the case of the India–Pakistan conflict is doubtful since no single actor—states, international or regional organizations or individuals—exercises such controlling influence over both governments, or enjoys legitimacy of the peoples to be able to perform its task successfully and effectively. A powerless mediator, or a mediator whose legitimacy is low, cannot achieve much.

There is a tendency to overstate the success of the US in crisis prevention between India and Pakistan during the Kargil conflict and after the terrorist attacks on the Indian Parliament in December 2001. However, as facilitation by the US and other Western powers was just one of the factors that resulted in the end of the Kargil conflict or prevention of war in December 2001, the external role cannot be given too much credit for crisis management in the region. Stephen Cohen has also cautioned against exaggerating the importance of the US role in bringing the Kargil conflict to an end.[28] As a commentator remarks:

> American diplomacy is having as much effect on India as President George Bush's admonition to Ariel Sharon earlier this year to withdraw his forces from Palestinian territory 'immediately', 'at once' and 'without delay'. If Bush cannot influence a country that the US subsidizes with more than $3 billion a year, why should the Indians and Pakistanis listen to him? If the US has no influence, what can little Britain or emasculated Russia do?[29]

Limited Success of Most Mediation Initiatives

In the majority of mediation attempts, the third party entered after armed hostilities had occurred, and its success was limited to bringing about a ceasefire. Most mediation attempts have failed to result in agreements between the parties. On the basis of quan-

[28] Quoted by L.A. Joseph, 'Posting an Untruth', *Outlook* (New Delhi), 9 August 1999.

[29] Charles Glass, 'Have We Learnt Nothing from Rwanda?', *Observer* (London), 9 June 2002.

titative data on mediation in the post-World War II period, Jacob Bercovitch states that only in about 7 per cent of mediation cases could a settlement be reached, while in other cases, mediation stopped with the cessation of war.[30] Another scholar confirms this conclusion when he writes that:

> The record of success of traditionally conceived intermediary activity is by no means a good one, especially at the international level. Powerful intermediaries tend to . . . impose settlements that prove to be temporary. . . . The world is full of abandoned, unsuccessful mediatory activities, and withdrawn or expelled intermediaries who have antagonized the leaders of one or more parties in a dispute.[31]

The end of the Cold War has not made third-party mediation more effective or successful. Peter Wallensteen and Karin Axell report that of the 43 disputes ending between 1989 and 1993, only 6 ended with a mediated agreement.[32] Roland Paris also argues that only one of seven UN post-conflict peace building efforts was successful.[33]

While cajoling the leaders for negotiations might bring about a ceasefire or short-term agreement, it does not repair damaged relationships or alter the nature of the conflict. The prime reason for the failure of mediation is the mediator's inability to address the underlying causes and structures which generate and accelerate the conflict. Such failure is also due to lack of understanding of the political, social and cultural context of the conflict on the part of the mediator, or due to the sheer fact of his being perceived as an 'outsider'. Mediators are also generally insensitive to psychological traumas, physical sufferings, and the self-fulfilling enemy images generated and reinforced by the conflict. The

[30] Jacob Bercovitch, *Social Conflicts and Third Parties: Strategies of Conflict Resolution*, Boulder: Westview Press, 1984.

[31] C.R. Mitchell, *The Structure of International Conflict*, London: Macmillan, 1981, p. 312.

[32] Peter Wallensteen and Karin Axell, 'Conflict Resolution and the End of the Cold War 1989–1993', *Journal of Peace Research*, vol. 31, no. 3, 1994, pp. 333–49.

[33] Roland Paris, 'Peace-Building and the Limits of Liberal Internationalism', *International Security*, Fall 1997, p. 548.

failure of the Lahore and Agra Summits—both organized due to American prodding—demonstrates that an externally-inspired peace process cannot last long, and that the conflicting parties get back to their habitual animosity once the external pressure eases.

Mediation can be Counterproductive

Mediation is not free from risks. As Jeffrey Rubin writes, 'mediation can also be an instrument of destruction if applied unwisely'.[34] Due to participation of the third party, mediation converts a bilateral conflict into a triangular one, making it harder to manage and resolve. Also, unsuccessful and unskilled mediation can lead to intensification of the conflict and worsening of relations between the disputants and the mediator. Considering the nature and intensity of the India–Pakistan conflict, formal mediation can further complicate relations between the two countries rather than making them more manageable. Failed mediation would also seriously call into question the credibility of the leaders of the two governments that invited international mediation, and even hold back bilateral negotiations for long.

THE PROSPECTS OF AMERICAN INVOLVEMENT IN INDIA–PAKISTAN CONFLICT

American involvement in and facilitation of the India–Pakistan dialogue process, as recorded in the earlier part of this study, does not constitute formal mediation. Even American policy makers refuse to call it 'mediation' in deference to Indian sentiments. However, the character of America's association with the India–Pakistan conflict has been facilitating and mediatory. As a premier Indian daily commented, 'the dictionary defines a mediator as one who acts as "go-between or peace-maker between two warring countries". Since going-between and peace-making are exactly the US mission on the subcontinent, the definition firmly places America in the role of mediator.'[35] There is no doubt that

[34] Jeffrey Z. Rubin, 'Models of Conflict Management', *Journal of Social Issues*, vol. 50, no. 1, p. 33.

[35] Editorial, *Times of India*, 12 June 2002.

America is interested in playing the role of an active peace broker in the subcontinent in whatever manner it can. However, for public posturing, it continues to maintain that it will not intervene as a mediator unless it is desired by both the concerned parties.

America's interest and involvement in South Asia have increased in recent times due to two reasons. First, the US attaches the highest importance to the control of nuclear proliferation in other countries, and, therefore, feels greatly concerned by the nuclearization of the subcontinent. Avoiding a situation that might trigger a nuclear war in the region remains its top priority for the region. Second, America's own strategic interests in Afghanistan and the Middle East in the aftermath of the terrorist attacks on 11 September 2001 have pushed South Asia higher up in its foreign policy priorities. The US has strong commercial and business interests in India, considering the investments that American multinational corporations have made there and the size of India's fast-growing market. The US also acknowledges India as a major player in world affairs in the coming years, especially as a counterbalance, along with Japan, to Chinese power in the Asian region.

America today enjoys better relations with both India and Pakistan simultaneously than it has at any time in the past. This also makes its involvement acceptable to both the countries. The suspicions and distrust that bedevilled India and the US during the Cold War era no longer exist. The two countries are on a firm route of cooperation and progress. Recently, cooperation between the two countries in military and strategic matters has also materialized. Its strategic location as well as the use of its territory and military facilities for waging war against the Taliban government in 2001 and for its overall fight against terrorism have also brought Pakistan back from a marginal status in America's regional strategy after the military coup of October 1999 to that of 'major non-NATO ally' status now.

The new bonhomie in Indo–American relations, however, has not removed irritants in the path of US facilitation of the India–Pakistan conflict resolution process. Indian public opinion is yet to be fully convinced about the honesty and even-handedness of America's role in the India–Pakistan conflict. Despite the evidence supplied by India, the soft approach of successive American administrations towards what India calls 'Pakistan-sponsored terrorism in Kashmir' has generated deep suspicion in Indian minds regarding America's commitment to fight all forms of terrorism. Indians feel convinced that the US can do more, yet is not doing enough to deal with terrorism emanating from Pakistan. By granting the status of 'major non-NATO ally' to Pakistan, the US has caused further erosion in its credibility as an impartial arbiter. Though the two countries share a common belief in democracy, India has failed to receive American diplomatic and political support in international forums. Instead, the US has supported a series of militarist regimes in Islamabad for its own political interests. The Musharraf regime, despite his having acquired power after a military coup and stifled democracy internally by keeping major political leaders out of the country, has also received profuse praise from US policy makers. Doubts have also been raised in some quarters that the US has a secret agenda on Kashmir, and that its involvement with the conflict is not as much out of genuine desire to defuse tension between India and Pakistan, but rather out of its own long-range strategic interests in Central Asia and China, where the location of Kashmir can be of great assistance. According to this line of thinking, the US role in India–Pakistan relations constitutes nothing but a form of imperialism and political control in the post-Cold War era.[36] Even some Pakistani scholars like Shireen Mazari have opposed the US role between India and Pakistan, because American mediation in international conflicts was ineffective, as its intervention could not restore peace in the Middle East or in Northern Ireland.[37]

Considering the above factor, observers believe that it is unlikely for the US to get involved to a significant degree and in

[36] Shastri Ramachandran, 'New Imperialism: Future Lies in the Past', *Times of India*, 29 July 2002.

[37] 'US Mediation in Kashmir Opposed', *Dawn*: http://dawn.com/2001/08/06/top8.htm, 6 August 2001.

a substantive manner in the resolution of the conflict between India and Pakistan. Sumit Ganguly, for instance, writes:

> The neuralgic Indian reaction to any third-party intervention in the (Kashmir) dispute is well-known. Nevertheless, the United States, contrary to the fears of many in New Delhi's policymaking circles, is unlikely to get involved without the explicit request of both India and Pakistan. In recent years, both Democratic and Republican administrations have stressed the importance of bilateral negotiations for settling the dispute. It is most unlikely that American policy on this issue will undergo a dramatic shift in the foreseeable future.[38]

The subtleties and complexities of the relationships between the communities and the countries of South Asia are best understood and handled by the people directly involved. Hence, instead of becoming an active mediator trying to solve the Kashmir and other disputes between India and Pakistan, the US should play the role of a facilitator. It can also extend assistance in establishing and strengthening democracy in Pakistan, as well as in ensuring that human rights and a democratic system in the state of Jammu & Kashmir continue on course undisturbed. It has also been suggested that the US can help revitalize Kashmir's economy and remove its backwardness by encouraging foreign investment and development assistance from international financial agencies like the World Bank and the Asian Development Bank. Key areas for investment are watershed development, the timber industry, fruit processing, and power generation.[39] This, of course, would require suitable legal and administrative changes in India.

PRIVATE AND UNOFFICIAL MEDIATION

Lately, civil societies have been playing a crucial role in conflict avoidance and resolution efforts. The civil society organizations employ a wide spectrum of approaches and non-formal methods

[38] Sumit Ganguly, 'The Start of a Beautiful Friendship? The United States and India', *World Policy Journal*, vol. XX, no. 1, Spring 2003, p. 29.

[39] Wajahat Habibullah, 'The Political Economy of the Kashmir Conflict: Opportunities for Economic Peace Building and for US Policy', Special Report 121, The United States Institute of Peace, June 2004.

of intervention to bring about reconciliation. Popular pressure and public education help the political leadership move forward towards reconciliation. A remarkable recent case of the efficacy of civil society's intervention is the settlement of the Irish conflict. Human rights groups, the Church, research institutes and private peace initiatives, etc., facilitated and strengthened the efforts of the governments to formalize a peace agreement. The peaceful end of apartheid in South Africa was also largely due to the participation of civil society organizations.

Empowerment and active participation of civil society are, therefore, essential for the success of a peace process between India and Pakistan. As the sources of this conflict are historical, societal, and psychological, it makes sense to search the potential of conflict resolution within the Indian and Pakistani societies. Some scholars and commentators, therefore, recommend private and indigenous mediation between India and Pakistan. Moonis Ahmar, for instance, suggests mediation by eminent personalities, retired officials, film stars, sportspersons, businesspersons, academicians and journalists or Track II organizations from the SAARC countries. He writes:

> What is required to promote indigenous mediation is to institutionalize the endeavours of the various private citizens, groups and NGOs of South Asia for peace building between India and Pakistan. Indigenous mediation is an option which should be tried by India and Pakistan because it is neither foreign motivated nor a threat to the interest of the two countries.[40]

Pakistani journalist and peace activist M.B. Naqvi has also advocated mediation by 'respected international, Indian and Pakistani persons' to resolve the India–Pakistan conflict.[41] The

[40] Moonis Ahmar, 'Gains and Costs of Third Party Mediation: A Case Study of Indo-Pak Normalization Process', unpublished paper presented at the international conference on Cooperation in South Asia: Resolution of Inter-State Conflicts, School of International Studies, Jawaharlal Nehru University, 29–30 March 1999, p. 14.

[41] M.B. Naqvi, 'Let Respected International, Indian and Pakistani Persons Mediate', *PUCL Bulletin* (Internet edn.), February 2000.

governments and bureaucrats, due to the logic of power and survival, are least likely to be ready to negotiate and settle with each other. Hence, it is the intelligentsia of India and Pakistan, joined by respected international personalities like Jimmy Carter, Nelson Mandela, Mikhail Gorbachev, etc., who can start a dialogue between the two governments.[42]

Private mediators are not burdened by the compulsions and rigidity that bog down political decision makers in conflict thinking. They have the freedom to experiment, be creative, and offer innovative solutions. Because the India–Pakistan conflict is a mix of domestic and interstate interests, private, non-official intermediaries may be able to influence the perceptions of the people, weaken the constituencies opposed to peacemaking, and help in preparing a conducive and conciliatory environment at the pre-negotiation phase of India–Pakistan dialogues. Private mediation might run parallel to official state-level mediation and supplement the negotiations between government officials and political leaders.

However, the question is whether such mediation by well-intentioned individuals and organizations without policy making roles can succeed. Private mediators have neither 'sticks' nor 'carrots' to induce favourable response from the two parties. The past record unmistakably points out that mediation by non-governmental individuals and organizations has the least chance of success. Such intermediaries 'fail even to have their offer of intermediary assistance considered seriously by parties in conflict'.[43] Also, as the interface between the official and non-official channels of peacemaking is not close in South Asia, the channelling of ideas and decisions of unofficial peace talks to the Ministries of Foreign Affairs and Defence is quite improbable. Unlike the US and other Western countries, the organizational structures of the foreign policy establishments in India and Pakistan are such that there is no scope for outsiders—private citizens, scholars, journalists, retired diplomats and others—to influence the official decision making processes.

[42] Ibid.

[43] Mitchell, *Structure of International Conflict*, p. 312.

Track II meetings can play a very useful function as a complement to official facilitation. Such meetings can sensitize common Indians and Pakistanis to the underlying conditions, ideas, misperceptions, political dynamics, and issues that make them each other's enemy. Such sensitization can slowly alter the parties' perceptions of each other, and awaken them to the need for mutually beneficial or integrative options of conflict resolution. Track II can also help neutralize the mental stereotyping that conditions perceptions of Indians and Pakistanis towards each other. Stereotyping is a process of assuming that a person or group has one or more characteristics, because most members of that group are thought to have the same characteristics. When stereotypes are inaccurate and negative (as they often are between groups in conflict), they lead to misunderstandings which make resolving conflict more difficult.

CHAPTER 6

Concluding Observations

At the time of Independence of India and Pakistan, Jawaharlal Nehru and Mohammed Ali Jinnah articulated the hope that the future relations between their nations would be cordial and non-adversarial. As Partition had proven to be a sort of catharsis for the centuries of accumulated communal tension, the age of independence was expected to be free from the historically inherited antagonism and rivalry. However, the happenings of the past 55 years have proven otherwise. The relationship between India and Pakistan remains an unending story of distrust, tension, violence, and conflict.

Any international conflict takes place in a systemic international environment. The relations between two nations and the measures they employ to control, mitigate, or resolve the conflict between them are not independent of such environmental variables. The nature and structure of the international system, and the overall normative framework guiding the foreign policies of the two states involved in the conflict are bound to determine these measures. Even as the India–Pakistan conflict has retained the same intensity and quality over the decades, the international system has experienced confounding transformations during the same period. A coalition of the economically and militarily powerful Western states led by the US dominates the international order today. This coalition is probably the most powerful coalition of states in international history, controlling international organizations, multilateral economic institutions, and advanced technology regimes. The modern communication system and globalization processes reinforce its supremacy. Based on shared cultural characteristics and a common ideological and programmatic agenda, this coalition defines the ordering mechanisms of the present world. Halting nuclear proliferation, maintaining the security of global trade, and promoting democracy are high on its agenda. Intervention in the internal or interstate conflicts in Asia and Africa in the name of defence of human rights, fight against global terrorism, and elimination of weapons of mass destruction have become all too frequent since the end of the Cold War to give comfort to the developing states. Such intervention makes the principles of internal and external sovereignties look old-fashioned. Considering that the threats of terrorism, violation of human rights and use of nuclear weapons are ever-present in the developments relating to the India–Pakistan conflict, involvement of this coalition of great powers in their affairs and accommodation of their concerns and priorities in the foreign policies of the two states seem unavoidable. It is unrealistic to expect that the other powers which matter in international relations will let India and Pakistan continue their conflict unabated.

Examining the applicability, performance and limitations of mediation in the India–Pakistan conflict, this study has argued that, notwithstanding the intrusive policies of the great powers, formal mediation in this conflict by any other state or international organization is unlikely and unappealing due to a host of reasons. India's consistent opposition to mediation for its own set of reasons, and its frustrating experience with the UN involvement in Kashmir rule out a formal third-party role. Besides, as analysed in detail in the preceding chapter, the contextual factors and antecedent conditions of India–Pakistan relations are unfavourable for mediation. The historical, social and psychological bases of this conflict as well as the nature of the issues between India and Pakistan are not amenable to a third-party role. The intermeshing of domestic factors with the external relations between the two states, the detrimental role of internal constituencies interested in the continuation of the conflict, lack of political will on the part of the ruling elite, and the low level of confidence between India and Pakistan make such third-party role exceedingly challenging and complicated. Besides, the asymmetry of military and economic power between the two states, coupled with the absence of a single actor enjoying coercive influence over them render international mediation unsuitable for this conflict.

Disputant motivation is the first requirement for the acceptance and effectiveness of mediation. The motivation for mediation is very high as far as Pakistan is concerned, because of the realization that it may not be able to get what it wants either through unilateral action or in a purely bilateral framework. Mediation could thus become a power-enhancing exercise for Pakistan. India has very low motivation for formal mediation, since it looks upon such intervention as a source of threat and weakness. Knowing fully well that in the post-nuclear phase any big crisis in India–Pakistan relations would make formal outside intervention inevitable and unavoidable, India has preferred to allow a facilitating role of third parties in crisis prevention, so as to avoid a bigger role for them in future in the event of a crisis getting out of hand. A total rebuff to the role of the US and other states like the UK in India–Pakistan crises would only alienate these powers from India and push them towards Pakistan.

However, the evident irrelevance of formal mediation in the India–Pakistan conflict does not point to the abandoning of a third-party role altogether. The function of mediation in this conflict has to be seen in broader terms as an interactive and extended process of facilitation and conciliation encompassing a diverse set of actors at several levels. Facilitation by these diverse actors—states, international organizations and non-state actors—should be regarded as mutually reinforcing and suitable at different stages. Formal mediation addresses the manifest symptoms of a conflict, and might be motivated by the interests of some powers. Informal conciliation and facilitation, on the other hand, have the latitude of dealing with the underlying sources and nature of this conflict. Multilevel and multi-actor facilitation have the potential to contribute to the improvement of the overall conflict environment. Even as third parties may be unable to influence the substance of negotiations, their role in communication and facilitation between India and Pakistan has to be put on a firmer footing. Such a facilitating and communicative role is a fait accompli and is going to remain an inescapable feature of India–Pakistan relations in future. Such a role should be carried out in a dynamic, continuous, and evolutionary way. The facilitators would have to see to it that the dialogue process remains on track, and the overriding common interests of both the sides are not lost sight of in a dialogue on the contentious issues. Also, rather than looking at the multilateral and bilateral tracks of negotiations in isolation, they should be applied simultaneously and in a complementary fashion.

An international conflict is a triadic phenomenon, consisting of three vertices, viz., conflict behaviour, conflict structure, and conflict attitudes. C.R. Mitchell later explicated it in a slightly modified form.[1] A conflict structure can be considered as a state in which two or more parties or entities perceive that they possess mutually incompatible goals.[2] It, thus, consists of conflicting parties; positions adopted by such parties, the relationship between them, and issues of conflict between them. Attitudes and perceptions are also critical in conflicts. Conflict attitudes can be defined as:

> [T]hose psychological states (both common attitudes, emotions and evaluations, as well as patterns of perception and misperception) that frequently accompany and arise from involvement in a situation of conflict. Conflict attitudes and perceptions are assumed to be factors arising through the stresses of being in a conflict, rather than factors fundamentally causing conflict, although extreme attitudes involving hostility, misperceptions and dehumanization of the opposing party will obviously exacerbate any dispute.[3]

Conflict behaviour means, 'actions undertaken by one party in any situation of conflict aimed at the opposing party with the intention of making that opponent abandon or modify its goal'.[4] When groups coerce, threaten or damage each other, they are involved in conflict behaviour. Conflict behaviour also consists of gestures and communication between conflicting parties. The resolution of a conflict does not represent a change in conflict behaviour alone. It also covers changes in the other two vertices, viz.,

[1] C.R. Mitchell, *The Structure of International Conflict*, London: Macmillan, 1981.

[2] Ibid., p. 17.

[3] Ibid., p. 27.

[4] Ibid., p. 29.

conflict structure, and conflict attitudes. Since all the three vertices of a conflict triad interact with and influence each other, a good conflict management and resolution strategy should pay attention to all the three dimensions of an international conflict.

It is easy to resolve or help resolve a conflict stemming from a clash of interests; it is more difficult to deal with a conflict that emanates from a clash of values or attitudes. The several cases of mediation in the India–Pakistan conflict discussed in this study have aimed at producing a settlement by altering the behaviour of the governments of India and Pakistan without addressing the socio-historical structure and the attitudes that shape such behaviour. They have been driven by the minimalist goal of firefighting at the time of crisis or serious break in relations, which has limited value. Firefighting cannot be expected to maintain peace in the longer term. Unless the mediation process relates to the underlying conditions of this conflict, and seeks to modify the fundamental constraints on India–Pakistan relations (historical memories, psychological stereotypes, enemy mythology, religious consciousness, contending ideologies of nationalism), the probability of its success is weak.

Such preoccupation with conflict behaviour and neglect of its underlying structures and attitudes stem from the fact that the theory and practice of mediation are rooted predominantly in the realist paradigm of conflict resolution, and carry its cultural, psychological, and ideological underpinnings. The discourse on mediation has been constructed by far on the power-centric and state-centric view of international relations. It looks at mediation as an attempt to resolve conflicts through a top-down approach of delivering peace to society by the state actors. Such a perspective furnishes a weak foundation for conflict resolution, inasmuch as it conceives mediation as an interest-maximizing activity for the states involved, rather than as a conflict transforming process in which, apart from the states, the civil societies and the individual actors also participate. The motive behind traditional mediation is not desire for peace, but self-interested pursuit of strategic stability through manipulation and coercion.

The India–Pakistan conflict is not just an interstate or intergovernmental conflict. It is necessary to look at both the inter-societal and intrasocietal processes in order to understand the true nature of the India–Pakistan conflict and find ways of managing it peacefully. Hence, apart from political and diplomatic means, the scope for social, cultural, psychological, and economic factors in the process of conflict resolution should be created. By following a wide gamut of state as well as non-state, political as well as non-political, official as well as non-official activities, an attempt can be made to transform it. Unofficial and non-state activities could play an important role in creating a conducive environment for political and diplomatic activities to make some headway.

Misunderstanding, mistrust, or misperception are the basic causes of aggravation of conflict between antagonists. Actions that reduce chances of such misperception and mistrust, soften attitudes and promote an atmosphere conducive to conflict settlement are essential. Only relationship building and conflict transforming third-party facilitation, rather than outcome-oriented, solution-imposing mediation has utility in the existing context of the India–Pakistan conflict. The prime objective of such facilitation should be to support processes that build a relationship of trust and goodwill between the peoples of the two countries, and make them realize the dangers of conflict escalation. Reconsidering their conventional conceptual framework and normative assumptions in view of the distinctive features of the India–Pakistan conflict, the facilitators should aim at altering the perceptions and orientations of political actors and peoples. This requires deep understanding of the psycho-political dynamics and historical determinants of this conflict. The facilitative approach, if pursued over the longer term, can help turn the basic quality of India–Pakistan relationship from zero-sum and competitive to accommodative and integrative.

If politicians, diplomats, and military officers alone are involved with it, the India–Pakistan peace process may not even take off in the real sense, as these sections have a vested interest in the persistence of this conflict. They lack imagination and motivation to break away from the inherited frameworks of thought and offer alternatives to enmity. Even if they are willing to make peace, the entrenched policy making structures, bureaucratic politics or jingoism of fundamentalist groups may not allow them to break radically from the past. Therefore, unless the imperative of transforming the attitudes and mindset of people is addressed, and the peace process is broadened to bring in the masses, the goals of peaceful India–Pakistan relations may not be realized. Without popular interest in peace, the collective interests of the political–bureaucratic–military class or popular stereotypes might not slacken. Starting from the periphery, a slow movement towards inducing such psychological and structural changes that make resolution of contentious issues easier should be made.

A conflict can be resolved only when some mutually consistent set of actions is worked out, and when all the parties involved in a conflict see the solution as fair.[5] *Conflict transformation* is also a form of conflict resolution. It means replacing conflict with positive relationships such as cooperation, satisfaction, empathy, and interdependence between parties.[6] Unlike *conflict resolution*, which denies the intractable nature of some international conflicts, or *conflict management*, which assumes that people and relationships can be managed as though they were physical objects, the concept of conflict transformation reflects the notion that the nature of the relationships between the people involved in the conflict change with the change in the nature of the conflict over time.

The experience of peace processes demonstrates that an incremental approach is more effective in addressing intractable conflicts. It may not be possible for India and Pakistan to have a comprehensive settlement of all their disputes. However, they can move progressively upwards by concentrating on issues which are least contentious, and where the possibility of cooperation, accommodation, and mutual benefit is the largest. Interestingly, even as the conflicting aspects of their relationship have received

[5] Michael Nicholson, *Conflict Analysis*, London: English Universities Press, 1971.

[6] I. William Zartman, 'Towards the Resolution of International Conflicts', in I. William Zartman and J. Lewis Rasmussen (eds.), *Peacemaking in International Conflict: Methods and Techniques*, Washington: United States Institute of Peace Press, 1997, p. 11.

unending attention from politicians and the media, the lesser-known truth is that the India–Pakistan relationship has never been only conflicting. The two countries have an impressive record of cooperation in various sectors.[7]

Peace in South Asia is to be interpreted and attempted as a dynamic, wide-ranging and multi-actor process rather than as a static event. In the words of Harold Saunders, '… the peace process is more than conventional diplomacy and negotiation. It encompasses a full range of political, psychological, economic, diplomatic, and military actions woven together into a comprehensive effort to establish peace.… Progress towards peace depends on breaking down the barriers to negotiation and reconciliation—the other walls.'[8] However, it is evident that India and Pakistan have not initiated such a series of steps to qualify them as a peace process.

There is no doubt that mediation is one possible approach to conflict resolution and transformation in South Asia. What too often happens, however, is that this one approach is seen as the only approach, leading to the marginalization and neglect of peace building on a wider scale. The present research has raised several issues concerning the forms, nature, and strategies of mediation, facilitation, and conciliation in India–Pakistan relations. Hopefully, future explorations on these issues would deepen and sharpen our understanding of the manifold dimensions of great power involvement, as well as non-official facilitation in the process of conflict management and resolution between India and Pakistan.

[7] See the chronology of cooperation between India and Pakistan compiled by Chetan Kumar in Kanti Bajpai, P.R. Chari, Pervaiz Iqbal Cheema, Stephen Cohen and Sumit Ganguly, *Brasstacks and Beyond: Perception and Management of Crisis in South Asia*, New Delhi: Manohar, 1995.

[8] Harold H. Saunders, *The Other Walls: The Arab Israel Peace Process in a Global Perspective*, Princeton: Princeton University Press, 1991, p. 3.

Bibliography

BOOKS AND MONOGRAPHS

Ahmar, Moonis, *The Road to Peace in South Asia: Lessons for India and Pakistan from the Arab-Israeli Peace Process*, Urbana Champaign: University of Illinois, ACDIS Project, 1996.

——, *The Road to Peace in South Asia: Relevance and Irrelevance of Middle East Experience*, Karachi: Department of International Relations, University of Karachi, 1999.

Aiyar, Mani Shankar, *Pakistan Papers*, New Delhi: UBS Publishers, 1994.

Appadorai, A. and M.S. Rajan, *India's Foreign Policy and Relations*, New Delhi: South Asian Publishers, 1985.

Azar, Edward E. and John W. Burton (eds.), *International Conflict Resolution: Theory and Practice*, Brighton: Wheatsheaf, 1986.

Bajpai, Kanti, P.R. Chari, Pervaiz Iqbal Cheema, Stephen Cohen and Sumit Ganguly, *Brasstacks and Beyond: Perception and Management of Crisis in South Asia*, New Delhi: Manohar, 1995.

Banerji, Dipankar (ed.), *Confidence Building Measures in South Asia*, Colombo: Regional Centre for Strategic Studies, 1999.

——, *CBMs in South Asia: Potential and Possibilities*, Colombo: Regional Centre for Strategic Studies, 2000.

Behera, Navnita, Paul Evans and Gowher Rizvi, *Beyond Boundaries: A Report on the State of Non-Official Dialogues on Peace, Security and Cooperation in South Asia*, North York: University of Toronto–York University, 1997.

Bercovitch, Jacob (ed.), *Resolving International Conflicts: The Theory and Practice of Mediation*, Boulder and London: Lynne Rienner, 1996.

Bercovitch, Jacob and Jeffrey Z. Rubin (eds.), *Mediation in International Relations*, New York: St. Martin's Press, 1992.

Bono, Edward de, *Conflicts: A Better Way to Resolve Them*, London: Penguin, 1991.

Burton, John and Frank Dukes, *Conflict: Practices in Management, Settlement and Resolution*, Houndmills and London: Macmillan, 1990.

Chopra, Pran, *India, Pakistan and the Kashmir Tangle*, New Delhi: HarperCollins, 1995.

Chopra, V.D. (ed.), *Studies in Indo-Pak Relations*, New Delhi: Patriot Publishers, 1984.

Cohen, Stephen (ed.), *The Security of South Asia: American and Asian Perspectives*, Urbana and Chicago: University of Illinois Press, 1987.

——, *Nuclear Proliferation in South Asia: Prospects for Arms Control*, Boulder: Westview Press, 1991.

Cohen, Stephen *The Structural Dimensions of Conflict in South Asia*, Colombo: Regional Centre for Strategic Studies, 1997.

——, *Emerging Power India*, New Delhi: Oxford University Press, 2001.

Deutsch, M. and P.T. Coleman (eds.), *The Handbook of Conflict Resolution: Theory and Practice*, San Francisco: Jossey-Bass, 2000.

Devbhakhtani, Sony (ed.), *Regional Cooperation in South Asia: Prospects and Problems*, Washington: The Henry L. Stimson Center, 1997.

Dixit, J.N., *Anatomy of a Flawed Inheritance: Indo-Pak Relations 1970–94*, New Delhi: Konark, 1995.

——, *India–Pakistan in War and Peace*, New Delhi: Books Today, 2002.

Galtung, Johan, *Solving Conflicts: A Peace Research Perspective*, Honolulu: University of Hawaii Press, 1989.

Ganguly, Sumit, *The Origins of War in South Asia*, Boulder: Westview Press, 1994.

Grover, Varinder and Ranjana Arora (eds.), *50 Years of Indo-Pak Relations*, vols. I, II, III, New Delhi: Deep and Deep, 1998.

——, *World Community and Indo-Pak Relations*, New Delhi: Deep and Deep, 1999.

Gupta, Sisir, *Kashmir: A Study in India–Pakistan Relations*, New Delhi: Asia Publishing House, 1966.

Haas, Ernst B., Robert Lyle Butterworth and Joseph S. Nye, *Conflict Management by International Organizations*, Morristown, NJ: General Learning Press, 1972.

Heimsath, Charles H. and Surjit Mansingh, *A Diplomatic History of Modern India*, Bombay: Allied, 1971.

Kapur, Harish, *India's Foreign Policy: 1947–1992: Shadow and Substance*, New Delhi: Sage, 1994.

Kargil Review Committee, *From Surprise to Reckoning: The Kargil Review Committee Report*, New Delhi: Sage, 2000.

Krepon, Michael and Amit Sevak (eds.), *Crisis Prevention, Confidence Building and Reconciliation in South Asia*, New York: St. Martin's Press, 1995.

Krepon, Michael, Khurshid Khoja, Michael Newbill and Jenny S. Drezin (eds.), *A Handbook of Confidence Building Measures for Regional Security*, Washington: The Henry L. Stimson Center, 1998.

Krepon, Michael, Jenny S. Drezin and Michael Newbill (eds.), *Declaratory Diplomacy: Rhetorical Initiatives and Confidence Building*, Washington: The Henry L. Stimson Center, 1999.

Krepon, Michael and Chris Gagne (eds.), *The Stability–Instability Paradox: Nuclear Weapons and Brinkmanship in South Asia*, Washington: The Henry L. Stimson Center, 2000.

Kriesberg, Louis, *International Conflict Resolution: The US–USSR and Middle East Cases*, New Haven and London: Yale University Press, 1992.

Miall, Hugh, *The Peacemakers: Peaceful Settlement of Disputes Since 1945*, London: Macmillan, 1992.

Mitchell, C.R., *The Structure of International Conflict*, London: Macmillan, 1981.

Mitchell, C.R. and K. Webb (eds.), *New Approaches to International Mediation*, New York: Greenwood Press, 1988.

Nayar, Kuldip, *Distant Neighbours: A Tale of the Subcontinent*, New Delhi: Vikas, 1972.

Sandole, Dennis J.D. and Hugo Vander Merwe (eds.), *Conflict Resolution Theory and Practice: Integration and Application*, Manchester: Manchester University Press, 1993.

Singh, Jasjit (ed.), *India and Pakistan: Crisis of Relationship*, New Delhi: Lancer, 1990.

Spring, Ursula Oswald (ed.), *Peace Studies in a Global Perspective: Human Needs in a Cooperative World*, New Delhi: Maadhyam Book Services, 2000.

Talbot, Ian, *India and Pakistan*, London: Arnold, 2000.

Thakur, Ramesh (ed.), *International Conflict Resolution*, Boulder: Westview Press, 1988.

——, *On Kashmir: The Roots of Conflict in South Asia*, Boulder: Westview Press, 1992.

Touval, Saadia and William I. Zartman (eds.), *International Mediation in Theory and Practice*, Boulder: Westview Press, 1985.

Vasquez, John A., Stanford Jaffe, James Turner Johnson and Linda Stamato (eds.), *Beyond Confrontation: Learning Conflict Resolution in the Post-Cold War Era*, Ann Arbor: University of Michigan Press, 1995.

Vayrynen, Raimo (ed.), *New Directions in Conflict Theory: Conflict Resolution and Conflict Transformation*, London: Sage, 1991.

Weinbaum, Maurin G. and Chetan Kumar (eds.), *South Asia Approaches the Millennium: Re-Examining National Security*, Boulder: Westview Press, 1995.

Wirsing, Robert G., *India, Pakistan and the Kashmir Dispute: On Regional Conflict and its Resolution*, New York: St. Martin's Press, 1994.

Young, Oran R., *The Intermediaries: Third Parties in International Crisis*, Princeton: Princeton University Press, 1967.

Zartman, William I. and Saadia Touval, *Resolving Third World Conflict: Challenges for a New Era*, Washington: United States Institute of Peace, 1992.

Zartman, William I. and J. Lewis Rasmussen (eds.), *Peacemaking in International Conflict: Methods and Techniques*, Washington: United States Institute of Peace Press, 1997.

ARTICLES AND PAPERS

Ahmar, Moonis, 'The Applicability of the Helsinki Model for the Task of Confidence-Building and Conflict Resolution in the Indo–Pakistan Sub-Continent', *Contemporary South Asia*, vol. 3, no. 3, 1994.

——, 'Gains and Costs of Third Party Mediation: A Case Study of Indo-Pak Normalization Process', unpublished paper presented at the international conference on Cooperation in South Asia: Resolution of Inter–State Conflicts, School of International Studies, Jawaharlal Nehru University, 29–30 March 1999.

Ayoob, Mohammad, 'South Asia's Dangers and US Foreign Policy', *Orbis*, vol. 45, no. 1, Winter 2001.

Babbar, Mariana, 'Bilateralism is an Indian Trap', *Outlook* (New Delhi), 22 June 1998.

Baharvar, David, 'Beyond Mediation: The Integral Role of Non-Governmental Approaches to Resolving Protracted Ethnic Conflicts in Lesser Developed Countries', *The Online Journal of Peace and Conflict Resolution*: www.triinstitue.org/ojpcar, issue 4.1, Summer 2001.

Bajpai, Kanti, 'Pathways to Peace in South Asia', *BIISS Journal*, vol. 15, no. 2, 1994.

Behera, Navnita Chadha, 'Kashmir: Redefining the US Role', Policy Brief 110, Washington: The Brookings Institution, October 2002.

Bercovitch, Jacob, 'International Mediation and Dispute Settlement: Evaluating the Conditions for Successful Mediation', *Negotiation Journal*, 1991, reproduced in the USIS Special Feature Service article 110.

Bercovitch, Jacob and Allison Houston, 'Why do They Do it Like This? An Analysis of the Factors Influencing Mediation Behavior in International Conflicts', *Journal of Conflict Resolution*, vol. 44, no. 2, April 2000.

Chari, P.R., 'The Mantra of Bilateralism': www.ipcs.org, article no. 220, 9 July 1999.

Dixon, William J., 'Third Party Techniques for Preventing Conflict Escalation and Promoting Peaceful Settlement', *International Organization*, vol. 50, no. 4, Autumn 1996.

Fisher, Ronald J., 'Methods of Third Party Intervention', in *Berghof Handbook for Conflict Transformation*, Berlin: Berghof Research Centre for Constructive Conflict Management, 2001.

Ganguly, Sumit, 'The Start of a Beautiful Friendship? The United States and India', *World Policy Journal*, vol. XXI, no. 1, Spring 2003.

Hoffmann, Mark, 'Third Party Mediation and Conflict Resolution in the Post-Cold War Era', in John Baylis and N.J. Rengger (eds.), *Dilemmas of World Politics: International Issues in a Changing World*, Oxford: Clarendon Press, 1992.

Husain, Ross Masood, 'Promotion of Inter-Government, Inter-People and Inter-Institutional Understanding in South Asia', *South Asian Survey*, vol. 2, no. 2, 1995.

Krepon, Michael and Mishi Faruqee (eds.), *Conflict Prevention and Confidence Building Measures in South Asia: The 1990 Crisis*, Washington: The Henry L. Stimson Center, 1994.

Limaye, Satu P., 'Mediating Kashmir: A Bridge Too Far', *The Washington Quarterly*, vol. 26, no. 1, Winter 2002–3.

Naqvi, M.B., 'Let Respected International, Indian and Pakistani Persons Mediate', *PUCL Bulletin* (Internet edn.), February 2002.

Nathan, Laurie, 'When Push Comes to Shove: The Failure of International Mediation in African Civil Wars', *Track II* (Internet edn.), vol. 2, no. 8.

Rajgopalan, Rajesh, 'Neo-Realist Theory and the India–Pakistan Conflict', *Strategic Analysis*, vol. XXII, no. 9, January 1998.

Rosenau, James, 'Security in a Turbulent World', *Current History*, vol. 94, no. 592, May 1995.

Ross, William H., 'Hybrid Forms of Third-Party Dispute Resolution: Theoretical Implications of Combining Mediation', *Academy of Management Review*, vol. 25, no. 2, April 2000.

Shah, Aqil S., 'Non-Official Dialogue between India and Pakistan: Prospects and Problems', *ACDIS Occasional Paper*, Urbana: University of Illinois, 1997.

Sundarji, Krishnaswami, 'Strategic Stability in the Early 2000s: An Indian View of a South Asian Model', in M.L. Best Jr., J. Hughes-Wilson and A.A. Piontkowsky, (eds.), *Strategic Stability in the Post-Cold War World and the Future of Nuclear Disarmament*, Dordrecht: Kluwer Academic Publishers, 1995.

Tahir-Kheli, Shirin and Kent L. Biringer, *Preventing Another India–Pakistan War: Enhancing Stability along the Border*, Albuquerque, New Mexico: Sandia National Laboratories, 2000.

Vohra, A.M., 'India and Pakistan: Towards Better Understanding', *South Asian Survey*, vol. 5, no. 1, 1998.

WEBSITES

www.stimson.org
www.rcss.org
www.outlookindia.com
www.indiatimes.com
www.timesofindia.com
www.expressindia.com
www.thehinduonnet.com
www.csis.org
www.brook.edu
www.iiss.org
www.dawn.com
www.indiapak.net
www.indianembassy.org
www.epw.org.in
www.acdis.uiuc.edu
www.satp.org
www.idsa-india.org
www.worldbank.org
www.flonnet.com
www.subcontinent.com
www.stratmag.com
www.incore.ulst.ac.uk
www.ccpdc.org
www.trinstitute.org/ojpcr
www.globalpolicy.org
www.mediate.com
www.adrr.com
www.crinfo.org
www.interneg.org
www.c-s.org
www.ipcs.org
www.sipa.columbia.edu/cicr
www.nyu.edu/cwpnm
www.apsanet.org/~conflict
www.cisac.stanford.edu

RCSS PUBLICATIONS

- *Defence, Technology and Cooperative Security in South Asia: Report on the Proceedings of the Tenth Summer Workshop* (RCSS, 2004)
- *Environment Development and Human Security: Perspectives from South Asia* (2003)
- *Terrorism in South Asia: Impact on Development and Democratic Process* (SIPRA, 2003)
- *South Asia and the War on Terrorism* (India Research Press, 2003)
- *Shaping the Future—A South Asian Civil Society Dialogue* (RCSS, July 2002)
- *Small Arms and Human Insecurity* (RCSS, July 2002)
- *SAARC in the Twenty-First Century: Towards a Cooperative Future* (July 2002)
- *Memories of a Genocidal Partition: The Haunting Tale of Victims, Witnesses and Perpetrators* (RCSS, July 2002)
- *South Asian Security Futures: A Dialogue of Director's Regional Strategic Studies Institutes* (March 2002)
- *Security and Governance in South Asia* (September 2001)
- *Globalization and Non-Traditional Security in South Asia* (September 2001)
- *Security in the New Millennium* (India Research Press, 2001)
- *The Simla Agreement 1972—Its Wasted Promise* (Manohar, 2001)

RCSS Newsletter

A quarterly bulletin, it publishes a brief report of RCSS activities, presentations at its workshops on topics of contemporary interest and news and programmes of the RCSS and its alumnae.

RCSS Policy Studies

35 Nuclear Risk Reduction Measures in South Asia: Problems and Prospects (Manohar, 2005)
34 Indo-Pak Conflicts: Ripe to Resolve? (Manohar, 2005)
33 Small Arms and the Security Debate in South Asia (Manohar, 2005)
32 New Nuclear Triangle and China's Role in South Asia (forthcoming)
31 Stability through Economic Cooperation in a Nuclear Environment (Manohar, 2005)
30 Multi-Track Diplomacy between India and Pakistan: A Conceptual Framework for Sustainable Security (Manohar, 2005)
29 The Role of Mediation in Resolving India-Pakistan Conflict: Parameters and Possibilities (Manohar, 2005)
28 HIV/AIDS as a Security Threat to India (Manohar, 2005)
27 Nepal's Maoist Movement and Implications for India and China (Manohar, 2005)
26 Elite Perceptions in Foreign Policy: Role of Print Media in Influencing India-Pakistan Relations, 1989–1999 (Manohar, 2004)
25 Nuclar Risk Reduction Measures and Restraint Regime in South Asia (Manohar, 2004)
24 River Water Sharing Problem Between India and Pakistan: Case Study of the Indus Basin Water Treaty (June 2004)
23 Christianity and Political Conflict in India: The Case of Gujarat (June 2002)

Fellowship in South Asian Alternatives (FISAA) Monograph

- Water, Power And People: A South Asian Manifesto on the Politics and Knowledge of Water (1997)
- The Nuclear Debate: Ironies and Immoralities (1998)

Others

- *Directory of Individuals and Institutions Engaged in South Asian Strategic Studies* (1998).